Troubleshooting
&
Repairing
Small Home
Appliances

Troubleshooting & Repairing Small Home Appliances

Bob Wood

TAB BOOKS Inc.

Blue Ridge Summit, PA

Notices

It is the intention of the author that the information presented is accurate and stresses the need for safety; however, because of the nature of electricity, neither the author nor TAB BOOKS, Inc. is liable with respect to the use of the information herein.

Also note that an electric drip coffee maker is an extremely dangerous appliance. Do not attempt to troubleshoot or repair this appliance without the prior approval and recommendation of the manufacturer.

FIRST EDITION
FIRST PRINTING

Copyright © 1988 by TAB BOOKS Inc.
Printed in the United States of America

Library of Congress Cataloging in Publication Data

Wood, Bob.
Troubleshooting and repairing small home appliances / by Bob Wood.
p. cm.
Includes index.
ISBN 0-8306-9912-0   ISBN 0-8306-2912-2 (pbk.)
1. Household appliances, Electric—Maintenance and repair-
-Amateurs's manuals. I. Title.
TK9901.W66   1988
643'.6—dc19   87-33520
                                           CIP

Questions regarding the content of this book
should be addressed to:

Reader Inquiry Branch
TAB BOOKS Inc.
Blue Ridge Summit, PA 17294-0214

Edited by Suzanne L. Cheatle
Design by Jaclyn Saunders

Contents

Index 259

Acknowledgments

I wish to express my appreciation to the Goodwill Industries of Phoenix, Arizona, for providing some of the appliances for photographic purposes.

Introduction

A number of manufacturers market the same appliance, and an attempt to cover them all would require a large volume indeed. All appliances operate basically the same way, however, and often can be repaired simply and easily with common sense and a basic understanding of the way the appliance works. Appliances either heat or run a motor, or do both, and when these principles are understood, repairs become rather easy. For this reason, if you are unfamiliar with these principles, read the Basic Electricity and Troubleshooting chapters before you attempt a repair. Note that Chapter 3 in particular contains troubleshooting guidelines applicable to all projects. For this reason the information is not repeated for every appliance in Chapter 4.

Usually the biggest stumbling block is how to get the appliance apart. This book was written, not to aid the technician, but to provide an understanding of basic electricity and to encourage confidence in anyone who has a few simple tools and a desire to repair his/her own appliances. On some occasions, the appliance might need to be sent off to a repair shop or even discarded altogether. In any event, though, you as a consumer will at least have a better understanding of your appliances, and you will not be apt to be overcharged by some unscrupulous repair shop or to throw away an appliance needing a simple repair.

1
CHAPTER

Basic
Electricity

Energy is the ability to do work, and electricity is just one form of energy. Our understanding of electrical energy is based more on what it does than on what it is.

In its basic form, electricity is of little use. To be beneficial, it must be changed into some other type of energy. Electric toasters and irons are able to operate when electrical energy is changed into heat. If current is applied to an electric motor, the electrical energy is changed into mechanical energy. The resistance of a filament in a light bulb causes the electrical energy to be changed into light. When the battery in an automobile is charged, electrical energy is changed into chemical energy.

With all its versatility, we can use electricity to control the comfort in our homes, to provide us with light, and to power a large number of household servants. Electricity is easier to use than other types of energy. It can be transported to great distances almost instantly. It is a clean form of energy and is as convenient as the nearest light switch.

To find the source of electrical energy, we must look at an atom (FIG. 1-1). All matter is composed of atoms, and atoms contain particles called protons, neutrons, and electrons. We are interested in the electrons. Generally, electrons are confined to a single atom; however, some can, and do, move from one atom to another. They are called *free electrons*. The atoms in copper, steel, and aluminum have many free electrons; consequently, these metals are good conductors of electricity, copper being the best of the three (FIG. 1-2).

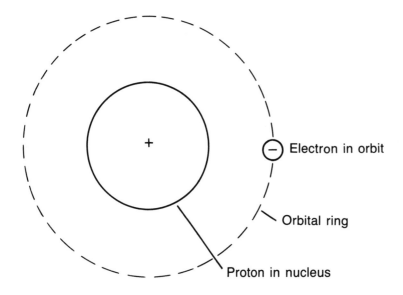

Fig. 1-1. Hydrogen atom showing one electron in orbit.

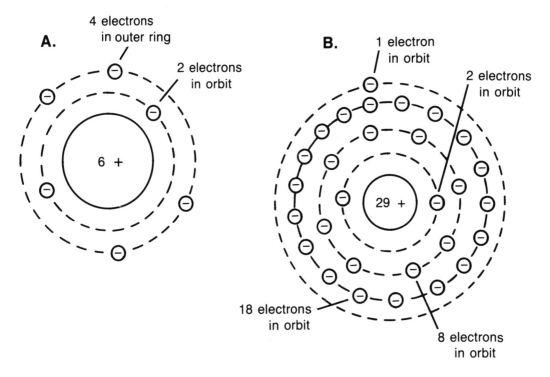

Fig. 1-2. Atomic structures of: (A) the carbon atom with 6 orbiting electrons and 6 protons in the nucleus, and (B) the copper atom containing 29 orbiting electrons and 29 protons in the nucleus.

The atoms that make up materials such as rubber, plastic, paper, and wood have little or no free electrons. These materials will not conduct electricity efficiently. They are called *insulators*.

There are two types of electrical currents. The one we use in our home and that is generated by the utility companies is called *alternating current*, or ac. The other, which is generally provided by batteries, is called *direct current*, or dc (FIG. 1-3). When the current flows in the same direction along a conductor or in a circuit, a direct current flows through it. Again, this type of current is generally provided by batteries, and in some cases by certain types of generators. If, on the other hand, the current flows first in one direction and then the other, the current is said to be alternating. These current reversals may occur at any rate from just a few per second up to a very large number, depending on the method of generation.

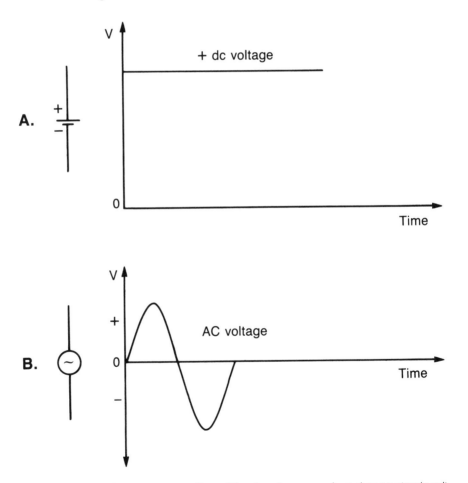

Fig. 1-3. A dc voltage vs. an ac voltage: (A) a dc voltage wave form shows a steady voltage with one polarity; (B) an ac wave form, often called a *sine wave*, shows the alternating voltage reversing in polarity.

Fortunately, a standard has been adopted for alternating current. Current flowing in homes and factories throughout the United States reverses itself 120 times per second. It takes two reversals to make up a *cycle* (FIG. 1-4). With this standard in use, all homes in the United States operate on the same frequency: an alternating current of 60 cycles per second. A frequency of 1 cycle per second equals 1 hertz (Hz). A current with a frequency of 60 cycles per second, then, is termed 60 Hz.

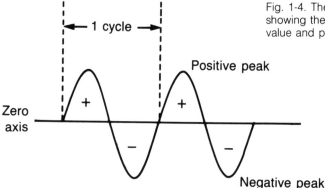

Fig. 1-4. The complete cycle of an ac wave form showing the constant changing in voltage value and polarity.

Batteries supply most of the direct current found around the home. They have the ability to convert chemical energy into electrical energy. Batteries come in two types: wet and dry. Electricity from the battery in your car comes from chemicals that are wet, whereas flashlights use batteries called *dry cells*. All wet batteries, and even some dry batteries, can be recharged from a dc source or battery charger.

A strange thing happens when current flows through a wire. A magnetic field is built up around this wire. Normally this field is very small, but if the wire is wound into several coils, the magnetic field of each one coil tends to add to the magnetic field in the next coil, and a strong magnetic field is quickly created. You might have detected the magnetic field of high-powered transmission lines on your car radio while passing underneath them. This annoying static indicates a strong magnetic field, but the phenomenon provides the principle for the operation of solenoids and electromagnets found in many familiar devices, from doorbells and auto starters to telephones and televisions.

An even stranger thing happens if we rotate a loop of wire between the poles of a magnet (FIG. 1-5). When this wire loop, or conductor, passes through the magnetic lines of force between the north and south poles of the magnet, a small current can be detected in the wire. Looking at the ends of a **U**-shaped magnet, we become aware of the invisible force around each end or pole, of the magnet. We can think of this magnetic field as containing lines of force emanating from the north pole and going back into the magnet at its south pole. The more powerful the magnet the larger the number of these lines of force.

Fig. 1-5. Electricity being induced, or generated, in a wire loop moving through a magnetic field: (A) current flowing counterclockwise through the loop in the first half of the turn; (B) no current flowing when the sides of the loop are not moving up or down; (C) current flowing again, but in the opposite direction.

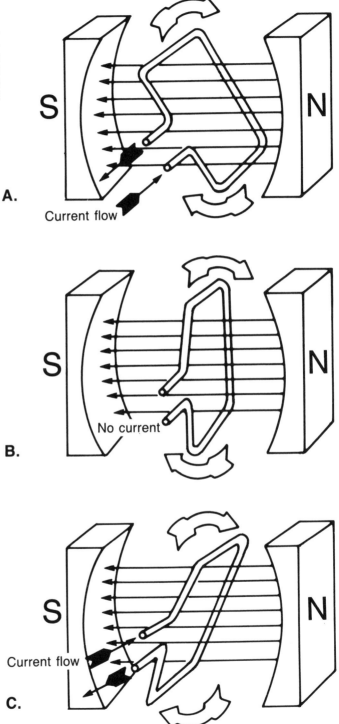

If we rotate a loop of wire within the magnetic field between the north and south poles of the magnet, the sides of the loop will cut the magnetic lines of force. This cutting action of the wire conductor through the magnetic lines of force is the phenomenon that induces, or generates, electricity in the loop. When the loop begins to rotate, one side passes up through the lines of force while the other side of the loop moves down. The current in this first half-cycle will flow in one direction. When the loop arrives at the halfway position and neither side is going up or down, none of the lines of force are being cut and no electricity is generated. As the loop continues on into the second half of the cycle, that part of the loop that was formally moving upward is now moving downward through the lines of force, and the side that was moving down is now going up. The current in the loop now flows in the opposite direction of the current induced in the first half of the cycle. When the loop again arrives at its vertical position, with neither of the sides moving up or down, again none of the lines of force are being cut and no electricity is being generated.

During each revolution of the loop, the current flows first in one direction, then reverses and flows in the opposite direction. Twice during this revolution there is no current flowing at all. This is the basic principle that produces alternating current commonly found in our homes today.

The voltage of this generator can be increased by any or all of the following: use of a more powerful magnet, which increases the number of lines of force, addition of more loops of wire that cut through the magnetic field, and faster rotation of these loops.

Electrical energy in our homes is supplied by the electric utility companies, which convert coal, oil, running water, or atomic energy into electrical energy. These utility companies operate huge generating stations that send electricity sometimes great distances to our cities and homes (FIG. 1-6).

To transmit electricity efficiently over long distances, it must be converted to a very high voltage with a low amperage. This is accomplished by transformers. The generating station feeds electricity to a step-up transformer which raises the voltage, and thus lowers the current. The electricity next flows to the high-voltage transmission lines, then travels the necessary distance to a substation, where it goes to a step-down transformer. The substation then delivers a lower voltage to the consumers in the area.

These consumers might be factories or industries that use a high voltage (480 volts and more). If, however, the consumer is a resident, then the electricity goes to another step-down transformer to provide the 220 or 110 volts supplied to the resident. If the service in your neighborhood is provided by overhead power lines, then you probably have noticed the canister-shaped devices on the power poles. They are the line transformers that lower the voltage to a manageable level for your home.

It is not often realized that, when you start an electric clothes dryer or turn on an air-conditioning unit, this increase in electrical consumption

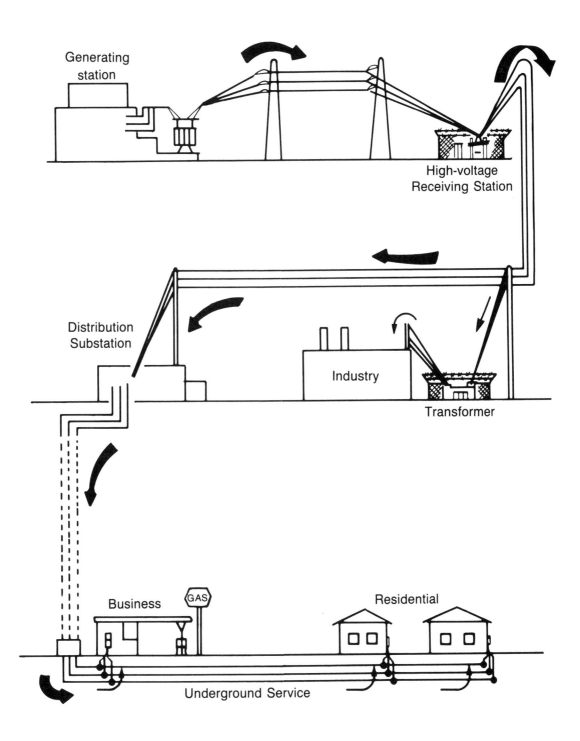

Fig. 1-6. Electricity usually travels many miles to reach our homes.

Generating station

High-voltage Receiving Station

Distribution Substation

Industry

Transformer

Business

GAS

Residential

Underground Service

is instantly seen at the generating plant, and their generators must respond with a larger supply of electricity. The energy of water can be stored in a reservoir or behind a dam, but electrical energy cannot be stored in large amounts. Therefore, the electrical utility companies must constantly maintain a small army of personnel and equipment to generate electricity the instant the demands are made. Usually a generating plant will have some form of generating ability on standby, for example, a generator turning that is not producing power. This standby source provides the insurance that, if called on, it can meet the need.

When we plug in an electrical appliance and turn it on, electrons flow from the generating station through the wires to the appliance and return back to the generating station (FIG. 1-7). The movement of these electrons is called *current flow*. The amount of current flow, or the number of electrons that pass a given point, is measured in units called *amperes*, normally shorten to *amps*. The force, or pressure, that moves these electrons is an electromotive force that is measured in *volts*. The work performed by the voltage and current is measured in *watts*.

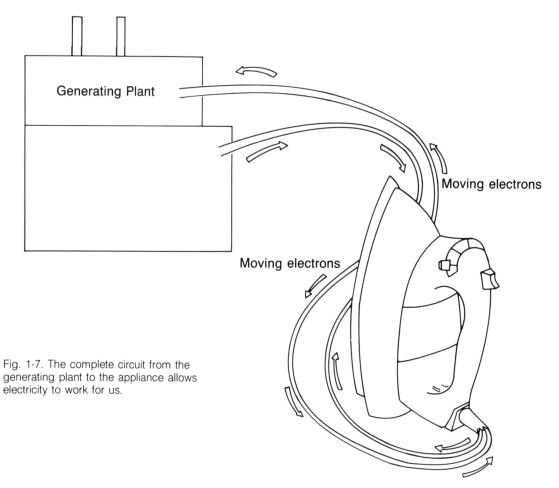

Generating Plant

Moving electrons

Moving electrons

Fig. 1-7. The complete circuit from the generating plant to the appliance allows electricity to work for us.

We can calculate these values by two simple formulas given to us by Ohm's Law (FIG. 1-8):

Voltage ÷ Current = Resistance

Voltage × Current = Power in Watts

Fig. 1-8. By covering one of the values in the circle, the remaining will be the formula for determining that value. For example, to find the current when you know the watts of power and the voltage, cover the **I** in the circle and divide the power by the voltage.

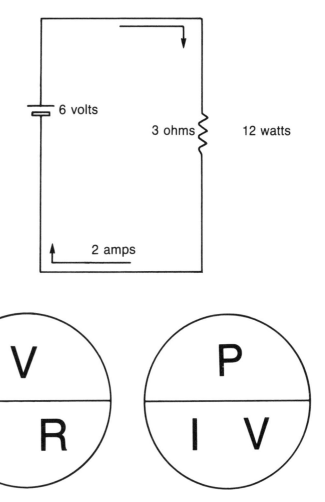

6 volts

3 ohms   12 watts

2 amps

P = POWER
V = VOLTAGE
I = CURRENT
R = RESISTANCE

The most important condition that affects the flow of electrical current is resistance. Electricity is selective about the materials through which it flows. As with any current, it will flow in the path offering the least resistance. This electrical resistance is a phenomenon similar to friction, whereby the larger the resistance, the smaller the current flow in the conductor. This resistance also has a tendency to generate heat. The resistance of a conductor is measured in units called ohms.

Most small appliances receive their power through two wires: a hot wire, normally black, and a neutral wire, normally white. Some appliances provide a third wire, or *grounding wire*, however, as a safety measure against shock. This grounding wire, normally green, provides a lower resistance to ground than the human body. When an electrical failure occurs in the circuit, electricity will flow through the wire to the ground, rather than through the human body to the ground.

We might think of the black wire as the wire supplying the voltage to the appliance, the white wire as the one returning it back to the generating station, and the green ground wire as a safety wire. Normally hot wires will be black, red, or blue. The return, or neutral wire, should be white or gray, and the grounding wire should be green or bare with no insulation at all.

To accomplish work with electrical energy, there must be a continuous path, or *circuit*, for the current to flow. It is sometimes convenient to think of electrical circuits as plumbing circuits and the electron flow as water. When the current travels through this circuit, it provides energy that can generate heat, create light, or make motors run.

Basically, an electrical circuit consists of a power source and a load (FIG. 1-9). The real source of power is the electrical company's generating plant, but for our purposes we'll consider the wall outlets in our home as the source of power. Our load can be broken down further into three parts. Generally it consists of a conductor, or the wires to the appliance; some switching arrangement, or power control; and the load of the appliance itself (FIG. 1-10). This could be a heating element, a motor, or a variety of devices from lamps, radios, and televisions, to electric razors

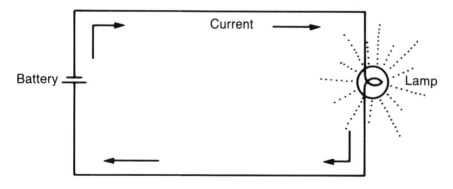

Fig. 1-9. The completed circuit will allow current to flow.

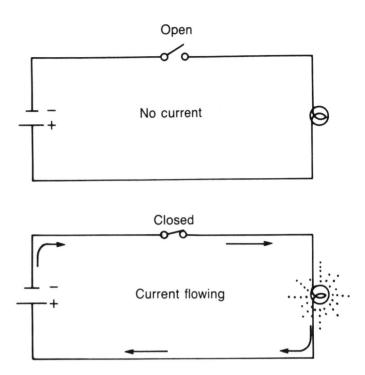

Fig. 1-10. Most electrical circuits contain some type of switching device to control the flow of current.

Open

No current

Closed

Current flowing

or telephones. The switch is simply a device that controls the flow of the current. In the analogy to water and plumbing, this could be the faucet to a sprinkler system in the lawn.

Because of the large volume of matter making up our earth, the earth is electrically neutral, consequently current will flow when voltage is applied to a wire or conductor connected to the earth, or ground. If this conductor happens to be the human body, severe shock will occur (FIG. 1-11). By following seven simple rules, however, you can handle electricity quite safely and easily:

• First and probably the most important, is never, never try to repair an appliance while it is still plugged in.
• Try not to work alone. Have someone handy who knows where the circuit breakers are and how to trip them.
• Don't just jump into a project; work slowly, stop and think. Determine if the appliance is truly at fault and not the outlet.
• If you must check for voltages on an appliance, make sure the appliance is turned off and unplugged. Then connect your meter with alligator clips. Plug in the appliance and turn the appliance back on. Making certain that when you turn the power back on, you will not jar or disturb anything that you have connected.
• When replacing any wires, always use the same size as the original one. If you are not sure of the size, take the old cord or wire with you when you buy the new ones. A smaller wire in the wrong place could cause a fire.

- After you have made the repair and reassembled the appliance, check for shorts with your meter.
- Always make sure your meter is working properly.

By far the greatest safety device we have is our own mind. Stop and think, work slowly, and if you are in a hurry, don't do it. Many appliances have safety interlocks. If you use jumpers to try to defeat these interlocks, it's like playing Russian roulette. Fuses and circuit breakers are protective devices. Don't cheat; repair the problem.

If you are in a position where someone has been shocked and they are still part of the electrical circuit, do not touch them with your bare hands. First unplug the appliance or kill the power. If this is not possible, use some sort of insulating device—a coat or a broom—to remove the victim from the circuit. Then keep the victim warm and give artificial respiration, if necessary, until help arrives.

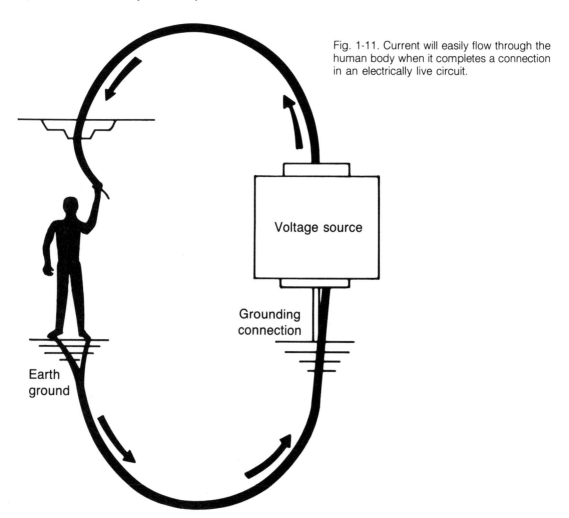

Fig. 1-11. Current will easily flow through the human body when it completes a connection in an electrically live circuit.

Voltage source

Grounding connection

Earth ground

2
CHAPTER

Tools

You will need a basic set of tools to repair small appliances. Most households have some tools already, but if purchases are necessary, it is important that you buy quality tools. A poorly made tool is never a bargain. A small-appliance home-repair kit should contain an assortment of Phillips and standard screwdrivers, along with a small set of wrenches. A soldering iron or gun also should be included with a supply of rosin-core solder. A roll of electrical tape will always be useful, as will a small assortment of wire connectors. Also, volt-ohm meters are not reserved for technicians. They have become very inexpensive and are extremely useful in troubleshooting, from determining the power levels of flashlight batteries to checking the continuity of electrical circuits.

It is important that you use the right tools for the right job. Don't use pliers when a wrench is needed. Don't use an adjustable wrench when an open-end or box wrench can be used. Using the wrong size of screwdriver might cause a screw head to be rounded out, making it almost impossible to remove the screw. These mistakes could cause an easy job to become very frustrating. Use a tool kit or small toolbox to keep your tools together and organized.

SCREWS AND SCREWDRIVERS

Probably the most used and abused tool around the home is the screwdriver (FIG. 2-1). It has been substituted for a variety of jobs requiring everything from chisels to punches; however, it was only designed to remove screws. If the square tip and corners become rounded off, it ceases to be a screwdriver. You can safely use a screwdriver to carefully separate two halves of a housing or to pry up a tab; just keep in mind that it was designed to install and remove screws.

Screwdrivers come in sizes measured in inches. A 2-inch screwdriver might have an overall length of 4 or 5 inches, but the business end, or shank, will be 2 inches long. Screwdrivers can be divided further into two classes: the standard, or flat-bladed, screwdriver, used for slotted screws, and the Phillips screwdriver, used for cross-slotted screws. A good home set will contain a variety of each kind, with sizes from 2 to 6 inches. Another screwdriver that is very handy to have around is the small jeweler's screwdriver. The removable shanks come in both Phillips and standard shapes. The handles on these screwdrivers are free to spin. This makes quick and easy work of tiny screws.

Another type of screw found in appliances has a recessed hexagon head. These are called *allen heads*. A set of allen wrenches may come with individual wrenches or in a pocketknife configuration; in any event, however, a set containing eight or nine different sizes will handle most allen-head screws (FIG. 2-2).

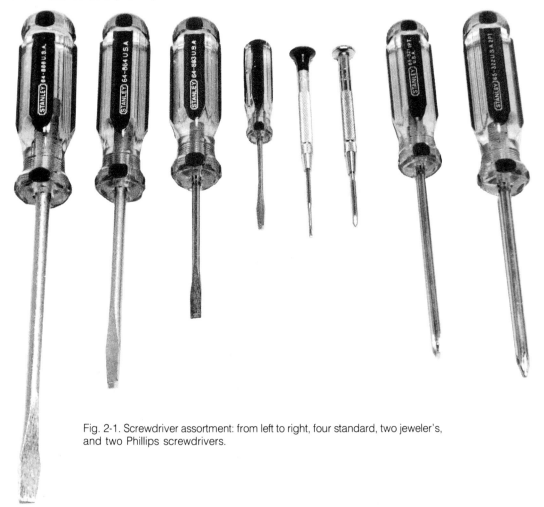

Fig. 2-1. Screwdriver assortment: from left to right, four standard, two jeweler's, and two Phillips screwdrivers.

WRENCHES

Nuts and bolts must be removed with wrenches, such as the open end or box wrench (FIG. 2-3). The box wrench completely surrounds the nut and provides a better grip. A set where both ends of the wrench are open will have a different size on each end. A set of 6 wrenches will handle 12 different sizes of nuts. A good size range in a set would be from 3/8 inch to 3/4 inch.

Another handy set of wrenches for the home is the socket set (FIG. 2-4). The socket wrench, like the box wrench, fits around all sides of the nut and provides an excellent gripping surface. The size most useful for homeowners comes with a 1/4-inch drive. The ratchet handle is extremely useful, particularly when a number of nuts of the same size are to be removed. These sets usually come with the extensions for the handles and fit nut sizes from 3/16 inch to 1/2 inch.

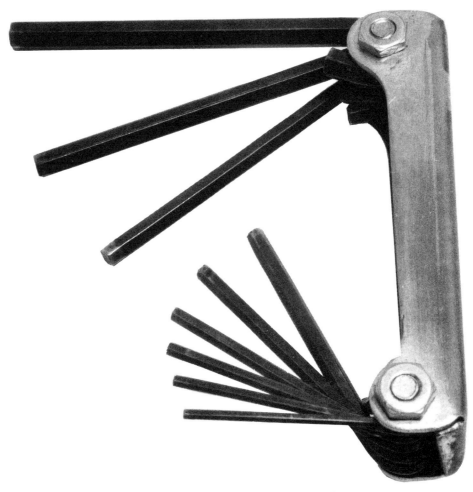

Fig. 2-2. A set of allen wrenches containing nine different sizes.

Fig. 2-3. A set of six open-end wrenches. Other types of wrenches include the combination open-end/box wrench and the box wrench.

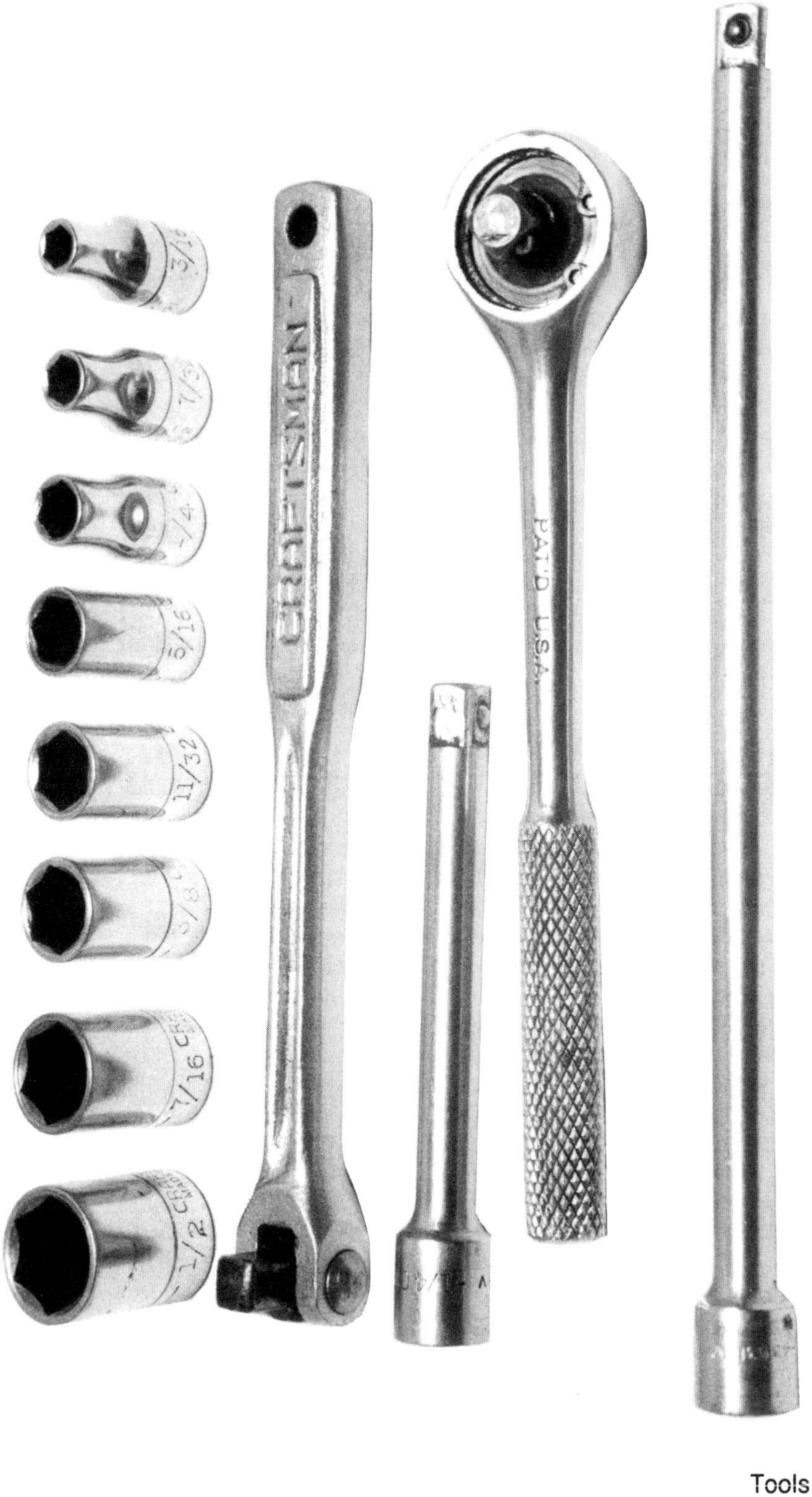

Fig. 2-4. A 1/4-inch socket set including the ratchet handle and extensions.

PLIERS

Needle-nose pliers are useful when you need to get into tight places where your fingers won't fit (FIG. 2-5A). A couple of different sizes will probably be all you need. These pliers also provide an excellent heat sink when you are soldering wires. (A *heat sink* is just a method of containing the heat of the connections being soldered to prevent damage to the surrounding area.)

TOOLS FOR WIRES

Because of the nature of electrical work, sooner or later, you will need a wire stripper (FIG. 2-5B). This tool is used for snipping off the end of a wire, then stripping the insulation from the end to make a connection. Developing a feel for when the insulation ends and the wire begins is the tricky part when stripping the insulation. The first few times, most people cut completely through the wire, but with just a little practice this task can be easily mastered.

A variety of inexpensive wire connectors are available (FIG. 2-5C). They provide good, solid connections without solder. Some, however, require the use of a crimping tool (FIG. 2-5D). A crimping tool is usually in the shape of pliers with jaws designed to crimp two different sizes of connectors. A small assortment of sizes of wire connectors and a crimping tool will be very useful in making electrical repairs.

SOLDER AND SOLDERING IRONS

Your toolbox also should contain a roll of electrical tape and a small supply of rosin-core solder (FIG. 2-5E). Small soldering irons are very inexpensive and available at most hardware stores (FIG. 2-6). The soldering iron, like any tool, comes in different sizes for different jobs. Soldering irons are rated by their wattage, and the larger the job, the bigger the soldering iron. The 25-watt pencil type that is illustrated is suitable for electronic work and light wiring, but is not capable of handling anything much larger.

In electrical work, always use rosin-core solder. Acid-core solder will corrode electrical connections. A rosin-core solder marked 60/40 is best. The numbers denote the ratio of tin to lead in the solder. Remember, the parts to be soldered must be cleaned down to bare metal. You can use a file or sandpaper to clean connections.

Before you attempt any soldering, you must tin the tip of the iron (FIG. 2-7). Simply plug in the iron and allow it to come up to temperature, then coat the tapered surfaces with melted solder (FIG. 2-8). Tinning prevents oxide buildup and helps provide efficient heat transfer on the tip. Eventually the tip will become discolored. When this happens and while the iron is still hot, wipe the tip clean with a wet paper towel or a damp sponge and retin it. When soldering a connection, heat the parts first, then when both parts are hot enough to melt the solder, apply the solder. The solder should melt quickly and flow evenly, coating all the

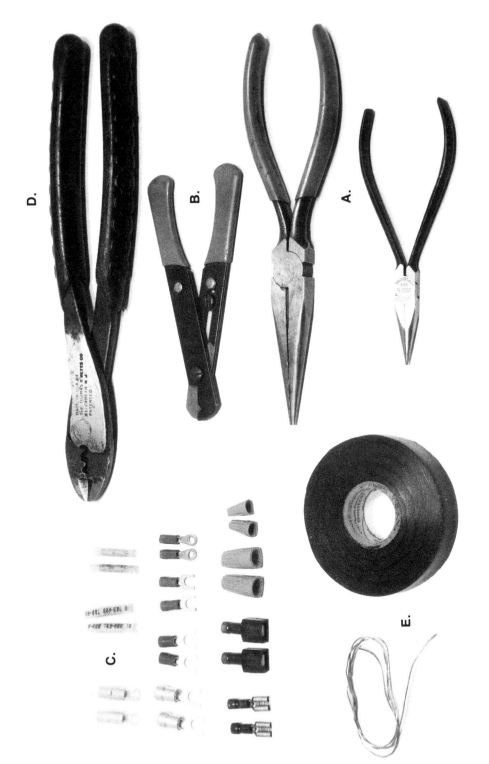

Fig. 2-5. (A) Two sizes of needle-nose pliers; (B) one wire stripper; (C) an assortment of wire connectors; (D) a crimping tool; (E) a small supply of solder and a roll of electrical tape.

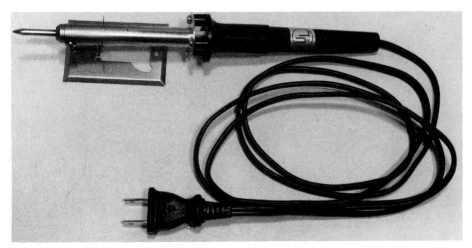

Fig. 2-6. A typical, inexpensive soldering iron.

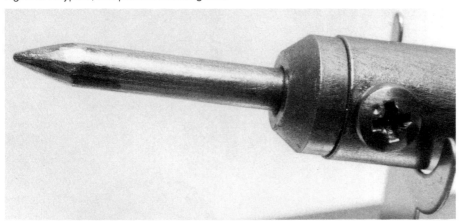

Fig. 2-7. A new tip must be tinned before using.

Fig. 2-8. The tip after it has been tinned.

20   Repairing Small Home Appliances

surfaces. If the connection has been heated enough, the solder will be smooth and shiny. If not enough heat has been applied, the solder will lump and may appear a dull gray. This is called a *cold solder joint* and makes a very poor, if any, electrical connection.

METERS

A small inexpensive volt-ohm meter makes a nice addition to the home toolbox and certainly makes troubleshooting small appliances a great deal easier (FIG. 2-9). The volt-ohm meter, or VOM, is primarily used to measure voltage and ohms, or resistance.

It is important for you to become familiar with your particular meter and the meter selector switch. This selector switch must be moved to the ohms side to measure resistance, and to the voltage side to read voltage. The voltage side is further divided into ac or dc. Next, you must determine the range or scale. You probably will need to refer to the instruction booklet that came with the meter the first few times you use it.

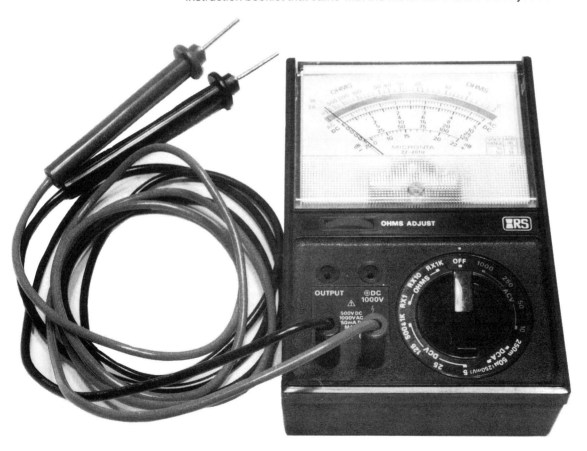

Fig. 2-9. A volt-ohmmeter is invaluable in any electrical troubleshooting.

By far the most useful purpose of this meter in small appliance repair will be to check for continuity, or resistance. To do so, move the selector switch to the ohms side and point to the highest or lowest range on the meter. These meters are delicate, but if not dropped or banged about, will provide years of service. The biggest danger to the meter occurs when it is connected to a live circuit with the selector switch pointing to the ohms side. Often the meter will be destroyed instantly.

Another useful meter is the clamp-on amp meter (FIG. 2-10). This meter, though primarily used to measure current, also will measure voltage, and has an ohm meter scale to measure resistance. This meter tends to be more expensive, however, and is probably better considered as a luxury item in the home tool kit.

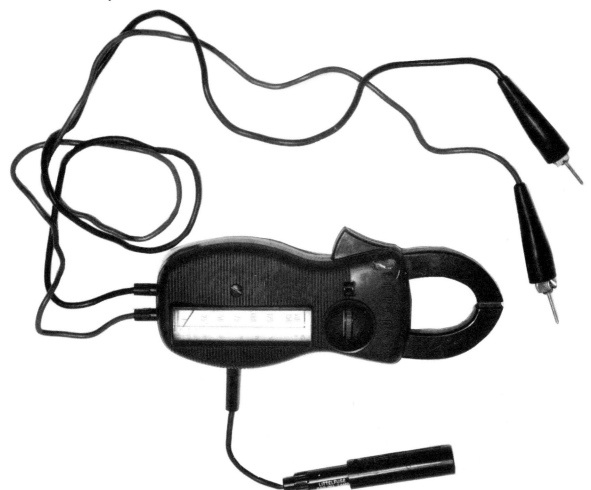

Fig. 2-10. A clamp-on amp meter indicates the amount of current flowing when the jaws of the meter are clamped around the wire. The lead plugged in the side contains a battery and fuse when the meter is used to measure resistance. One of the leads can be unplugged from the bottom and plugged back into the battery/fuse housing.

MISCELLANEOUS TOOLS

An old toothbrush and a small paintbrush are handy additions to the tool kit. They are very effective at removing lint and debris from small crevices in the appliances. A can of WD-40 or similar lubricant is useful to free stuck switches, as well as bearings on motor shafts.

There is a tremendous assortment of tools on the market today, and some appliance manufacturers use fasteners that require special tools to discourage anyone other than a factory service shop from making repairs. The tools covered here represent a good basic set and should be enough to repair most any small appliance. Any special tool can be purchased on an as-needed basis.

CARE OF TOOLS

It is important to keep your tools all in one spot where you can easily find them. Even the best tool is of no help if it has been misplaced.

A quality set of tools should be kept clean. It is very disturbing to pick up a screwdriver only to discover something sticky on the handle. A few drops of light oil on a soft cloth makes an excellent tool-cleaning rag. Simply wipe the tools after each use. The oil will help protect the metal parts from rusting. Tools have a way of disappearing if they are not returned to the toolbox after each use, so keep track of your tools, and they will be there when you need them. With just a little care they will last you a lifetime.

3
CHAPTER

Trouble~
shooting

When you purchase a new appliance, immediately mail in any warranty cards and place any remaining paperwork in a file. Don't throw any papers away; you probably will need them later.

There is a strong temptation to panic and call the electrician or plumber at the first sign of a problem; however, you should go slowly and check it out. There is a good chance you can make the repair yourself. Most problems are simple if you can get to the source. To consistently make effective repairs you must understand the operational principles of the appliance. Once you have a good grasp of how and why it works, the repairs themselves become second nature and are quite obvious.

Electricity is brought to our residence by three wires: two hot wires and one neutral. The wires are connected to the meter provided by the utility company, then brought to the service entrance panel on our homes. The two hot wires then travel to a main breaker, while the neutral wire goes to a neutral busbar. The busbar is connected to some grounded object—for example an underground water pipe or a long copper stake driven into the ground—to provide a permanent ground, an electrical path to earth, for your entire electrical system. The two hot wires connected to the main disconnect feed two other wires that go to two hot busbars. Individual circuit breakers will be fitted to these busbars for the various circuits in your home. These circuit breakers will be rated for 15 or 20 amps, depending on the service the circuit will provide.

A typical kitchen circuit might look like the one illustrated in FIG. 3-1. A good overall understanding of your power source is important in diagnosing any household appliance problems.

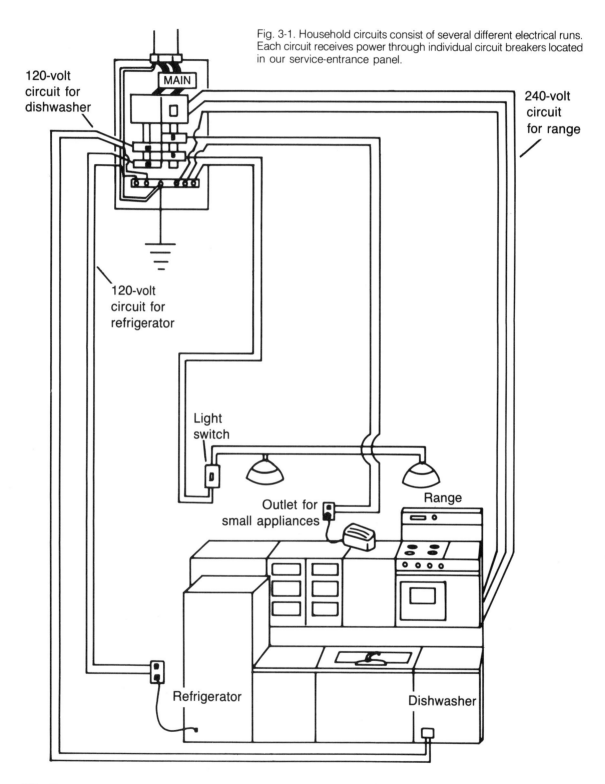

Fig. 3-1. Household circuits consist of several different electrical runs. Each circuit receives power through individual circuit breakers located in our service-entrance panel.

120-volt circuit for dishwasher

240-volt circuit for range

120-volt circuit for refrigerator

Light switch

Outlet for small appliances

Range

Refrigerator

Dishwasher

When you are trying to find the problem in an uncooperative appliance, always begin at the wall outlet. Determine first if it is getting power. If there is no power to the appliance, before you do anything, make sure you are plugged into a good receptacle or outlet. Plug a small lamp into the outlet and make sure you have power there.

The next place to look for a problem would be the power cord and the switch or control knob. Is it turned on? If the device is turned on and it is trying to operate, it might be a mechanical problem; that is, a gear binding or a motor going bad.

At this point you can usually determine whether it is an electrical or mechanical problem. If the problem seems to be electrical, then make a continuity test. Place the meter's selector switch to the *R x 1* position on the ohms scale, then connect the leads to the appliance plug (after briefly touching the leads together to test the meter) and turn on the appliance switch. If there is no reading on the meter, go to the highest ohms scale. If there is still no response from the meter, check the internal wire connections.

If the appliance heats, it probably has a thermostat. You might want to check it. Next on the list would be the heating element itself. If the appliance has a motor, take a look at the brushes. By checking probable causes in a logical order, you can find and repair most problems in a few minutes.

Keep in mind the job the manufacturer intended for the appliance to do. Was the appliance basically designed to heat, run a motor, or both? Normally, that's all our appliances do.

As with any repair, at some point you will need to determine if it is cost effective. Before you discard an appliance, however, make a simple inspection. It might reveal a problem easily repaired, not to mention giving you the satisfaction of doing it yourself.

The biggest aid to troubleshooting is reasoning. What is the appliance not doing, and why? Usually an appliance will malfunction for one reason only. Normally there will not be two problems.

PROBLEMS WITH CORDS AND PLUGS

By far, the most common malfunction on small appliances is caused by a faulty line cord or plug. The constant flexing and abuse causes them to wear quickly. Some of the danger signs relating to cords and plugs include burnt marks around the plug, intermittent operation of the appliance, and physical damage where the cord is badly frayed or the insulation is brittle. In these cases, the cord should be thrown away and replaced, not repaired. Excessive heat where the cord or plug is warm to touch is an indication of approaching problems.

Most small appliance plugs have two prongs (FIG. 3-2), but some will have three (FIG. 3-3). The third prong will have a different shape. It is the ground connection. Another plug that might need attention is called the *appliance plug* (FIG. 3-3B).

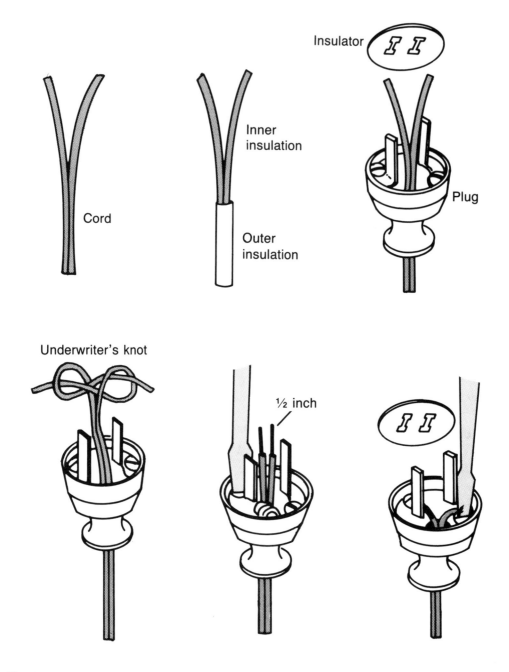

Fig. 3-2. To install a new plug, separate the cord about 2 inches. If there is an outer insulation, it will have to be removed first. Next slip the cord through the plug and tie an Underwriters knot in the cord. Strip off about ½ inch of the insulation and loosen—don't remove—the terminal screws. Twist each of the stripped ends clockwise, then wrap each wire, also clockwise, around the terminal screws and tighten.

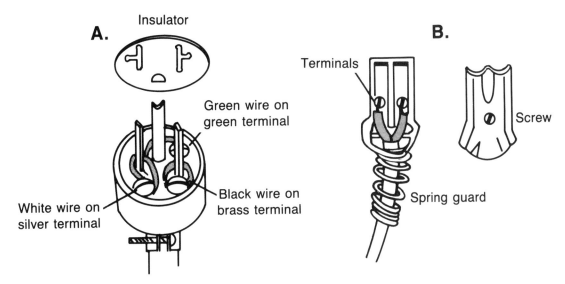

A.

Insulator

Green wire on
green terminal

White wire on
silver terminal

Black wire on
brass terminal

B.

Terminals

Screw

Spring guard

Fig. 3-3. (A) A typical three-prong plug and (B) an appliance plug.

Take a look at the plug and receptacle itself. Is one prong larger than the other (FIG. 3-4)? If so, the smaller prong or slot is the hot or live one.

Fig. 3-4. Some plugs are intended to be used only one way and have one prong wider than the other. In such cases, connect the small slot to the black, or hot wire. The neutral wire is connected to the terminal of the larger slot.

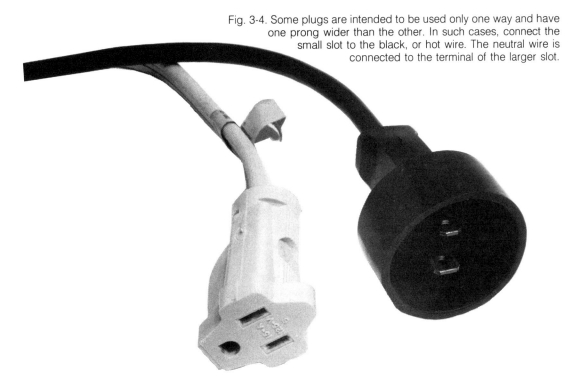

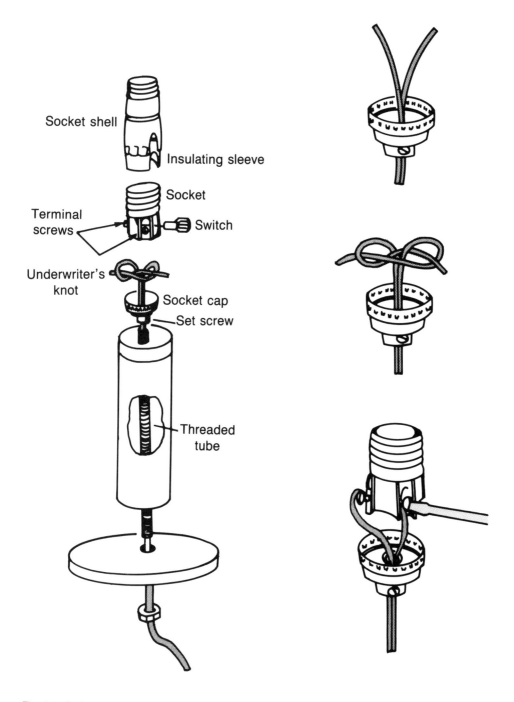

Socket shell

Insulating sleeve

Socket

Terminal screws

Switch

Underwriter's knot

Socket cap

Set screw

Threaded tube

Fig. 3-5. To install a new lamp socket, slip the cord through the socket cap, tie the Underwriter's knot, strip ½ inch of insulation from the ends of the wire, and twist each end clockwise. Next loosen—don't remove—the terminal screws. Then wrap each wire clockwise around the screws and tighten.

It is surprising the number of faulty plugs that go unattended, when it only takes a few minutes to replace them. Lamp sockets fail about as often as plugs (FIG. 3-5), but they are also easy to replace. Power cords might vary slightly in size and shape, but in order for them to be flexible only stranded wire is used.

You can discover a broken plug or loose prong by a simple inspection. A broken wire, however, might require some testing with a meter. The most common problem would be a broken wire inside the plug, which is caused by the constant flexing of the wire where it joins the plug. Flexing the wire with a meter connected to the plug might be the only way you can locate this problem.

It is always better to replace broken wires with new ones; however, it sometimes might be necessary to splice a wire. This splice must be strong enough that it will not pull apart, as well as make a good electrical connection. After the wires are twisted together, solder the splice and wrap it with electrical tape. Another choice, if you have a crimping tool, would be the insulated butt connectors. Insulated wire nuts are also available (FIG. 3-6).

Fig. 3-6. Wire nuts make good connections. Simply slip them over the bare ends and twist clockwise until tight. Then pull each wire separately to make sure the connection is secure.

TAKING THE APPLIANCE APART

Often, more time will be spent on getting an appliance apart than in making the repair itself. Some manufacturers go to great lengths to conceal the way their appliances are assembled. Sometimes screws are hidden under name plates in such a way that when a name plate is removed it cannot be put back neatly and the appearance of the appliance is destroyed. Screws might be recessed or hidden under felt or rubber feet. The control knobs usually can be pried off, but first check for set screws. If the knob refuses to move right away or easily, a retaining screw might be hidden under a metal plate on the top of the knob.

A connection to a switch might be made at a screw terminal, but more often it will be made to a self-locking terminal. If the connection is to a self-locking terminal, you will usually be able to replace the switch quickly and easily (FIGS. 3-7 AND 3-8).

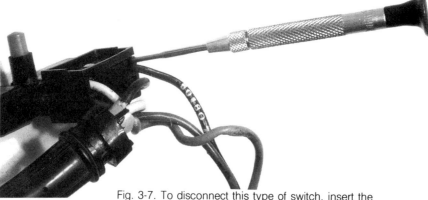

Fig. 3-7. To disconnect this type of switch, insert the tip of a jeweler's screwdriver or paper clip into the switch alongside the wire.

Fig. 3-8. Use the tip of the screwdriver to open the terminal, then you can remove the wire easily.

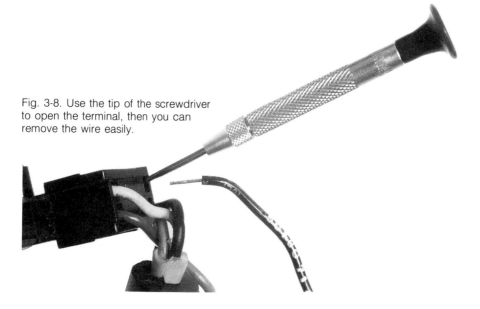

In disassembling an appliance, always remember to take your time. Set the removed parts aside in the order that they came apart, so you can reassemble easier. In some cases a rough drawing or sketch might be in order.

It is often helpful to mark internal parts with a screwdriver. Simply make a light scratch across two halves of an assembly. Often parts can only be assembled one way. If not, however, the light scratch will help you determine the correct positions.

When you are putting the appliance back together, check to make sure you do not pinch any of the electrical wires in the housing. Normally the wires have a different channel, or route, and unless the wires are put in their proper place, the cover of the appliance probably will not fit.

It is also a good idea to make sure all electrical connections are clean and tight. A corroded terminal will build up heat and resistance until it eventually fails. All appliances have some sort of strain relief inside the housing that protects the connections to the cord. The strain relief might be nothing more than a simple knot. Always make sure it is in place (FIGS. 3-9 AND 3-10).

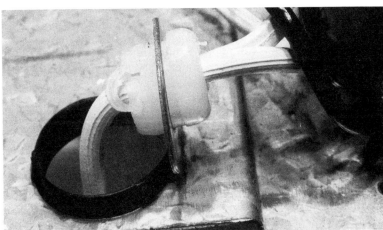

Fig. 3-9. Strain reliefs keep the line cord from being pulled from its connections inside the appliance.

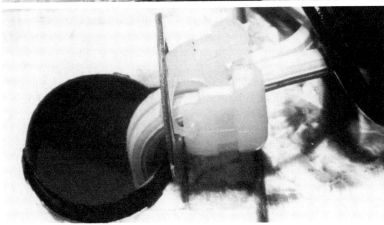

Fig. 3-10. You can quickly remove the strain relief by squeezing it together with pliers.

Always remember to use a minimal amount of force when you are taking appliances apart and reassembling them. After the obvious screws are removed, if the cover still does not want to come off, check for hidden screws or retaining clips you might have overlooked. Some design engineers are geniuses when it comes to hiding attaching devices. Some sections might need to be rotated or slid sideways to be removed.

HEATING ELEMENTS

When current flows in a wire, there is always some opposition to this electron movement. This opposition, or resistance, converts some of the electron's energy into heat. This is the basic principle in the design of heating elements in appliances. A heating element is simply a conductor with built-in resistance, designed to generate heat. These elements, often made of a nickel-chromium alloy called *nichrome,* have the electrical- and heat-resistant characteristics needed for the heating element to work. The wire or element itself will have a high melting point. The amount of heat the element produces depends on the number of watts the element uses, varying from 500 to 5,000. Elements generally differ from one appliance to the other only in the size of the elements. It follows that appliances with a higher wattage capacity will draw more electricity to create heat than those with a lower capacity.

The current to a given heater can be determined by the amount of wattage of the appliance. For example, a heater rated at 1,200 watts on 120 volts (divide voltage into watts) will draw approximately 10 amps. A 2,500-watt heater will draw nearly 21 amps.

Heating elements come in a variety of sizes and shapes, but they all do the same thing, basically the same way. Some come in the form of a heating coil enclosed in a ceramic-lined steel tube. They usually heat food directly, and the tube provides the protection from grease on the conductor. An electric stove, frying pan, and some broilers use this type of coil. Toasters and hair dryers use an element made from a wire wound on a flat mica insulator. This is a resistance wire and is wound in such a manner that is close to, but does not touch, what it is heating. Another type of heating element is called a rope-type element, and is nothing more than resistance wire wrapped in fiberglass insulation. This type is commonly found in the warming elements in coffee makers. You can use a meter to quickly check for continuity (FIG. 3-11).

There are two methods used to control the heat levels achieved by these elements. Generally, when an element is on, the heat output is fixed and is determined by the size of the element itself. The simplest method simply switches the heat on and off for an average heat output. After the desired temperature is reached, it is then controlled by a fixed or adjustable temperature thermostat. The other method of control incorporates a tapped heating element, where a connection to the element is made through a switch regulating the flow of current. These switches generally have settings such as low, medium, and high, and each switch position supplies a different amount of power to each given point in the heating element, thus producing a different level of heat.

A thermostat is simply a switch that automatically turns the power to the element on and off. This switching action stabilizes the temperature within a few degrees. In its simplest form, a thermostat consists of nothing more than a bimetal blade. Two strips of metal of two unlike alloys are fused together to form this blade. When heated, one of the metals has a high rate of expansion, and the other has a low rate. These differing expansion rates cause the blade to bend and then return to its normal shape when the heat is removed.

This bending or warping action is what opens and closes the electrical contacts. For example, if we place one of these bimetal blades near the heating element, then turn the switch on, the element begins to heat up, raising the temperature in the bimetal blade. This in turn

Fig. 3-11. This heating element checks okay. The meter is reading about 13 ohms on the R x 1 scale.

causes the blade to bend, which opens the contacts (FIG. 3-12), then the heating element begins to cool off. As the blade cools, it returns to its original position, closing the contacts and causing the current to flow again (FIG. 3-13), thus starting the cycle again.

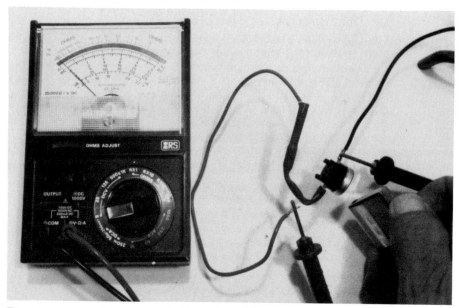

Fig. 3-12. Normally this thermostat will be closed, allowing current to flow, but the heat from a lighter causes the needle on the meter to indicate the thermostat is open.

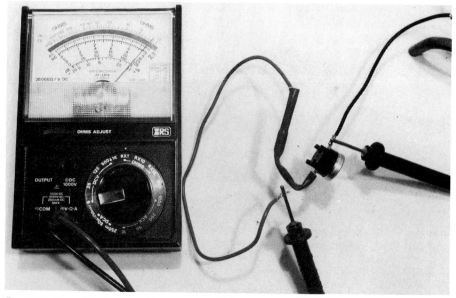

Fig. 3-13. When the thermostat has cooled sufficiently, the contacts inside come back together and the current is again able to flow through the thermostat.

MOTORS

The other common device in home appliances is a small electric motor. Basically two kinds are used: one with brushes and one without. *Brushes* are the little spring-loaded carbon blocks that make an electrical contact inside the motor. This type of motor is called a *universal motor* because it will run on ac or dc (FIG. 3-14). These motors are used in appliances such as food mixers and blenders, and generally whenever a high torque and possibly a variable speed are necessary.

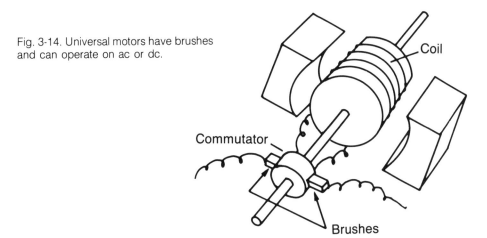

Fig. 3-14. Universal motors have brushes and can operate on ac or dc.

Coil

Commutator

Brushes

Another small motor in use is called a *shaded-pole motor* (FIG. 3-15). It operates on ac only and does not use brushes. These motors are used in appliances that require little starting torque such as clocks, fans, and hair dryers. These motors seldom cause any problems, but when a problem does occur it usually can be solved with simple cleaning and lubrication.

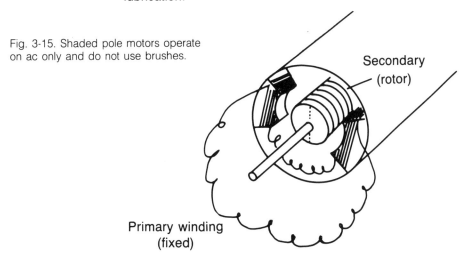

Fig. 3-15. Shaded pole motors operate on ac only and do not use brushes.

Secondary
(rotor)

Primary winding
(fixed)

On universal motors, problems sometimes occur in or around the brushes. Generally, however, the problem can be found in what the motor is connected to, such as a gear or a bearing.

One component that might be found in small appliances is called a *bridge rectifier,* which is usually nothing more than four diodes and a couple of capacitors mounted on a small printed circuit board (FIG. 3-16). Simply put, the rectifier changes ac to dc. The diodes act like valves and allow current to flow in only one direction (FIGS. 3-17 AND 3-18). So if the diodes are connected in such a manner that the current flows through two diodes on one half cycle then through the other two diodes on the other half cycle, what comes out is a *pulsating dc current.* This means that the voltage level rises and falls in cycles. The two capacitors (FIG. 3-19) are there to minimize this rise and fall, and thereby produce a reasonably level dc voltage.

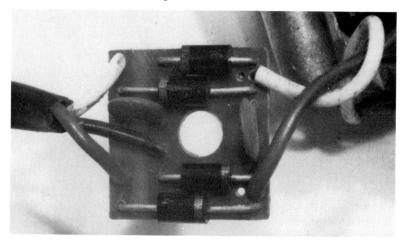

Fig. 3-16. (*above left*) A bridge recitifer mounted on a small printed circuit board. Rectifiers change alternating current to direct current. A "bridge" rectifier employs four diodes (rectifiers).

Fig. 3-17. (*left*) Diodes can be checked with a meter. With the negative lead of the meter connected to the end of the diode without the band and the positive lead connected to the other end, the meter indicates continuity. Current will flow.

Fig. 3-18. Turning the diode around and connecting the negative meter lead to the end of the diode with the band and the positive lead to the other end will produce an open reading on the meter. Current will not flow.

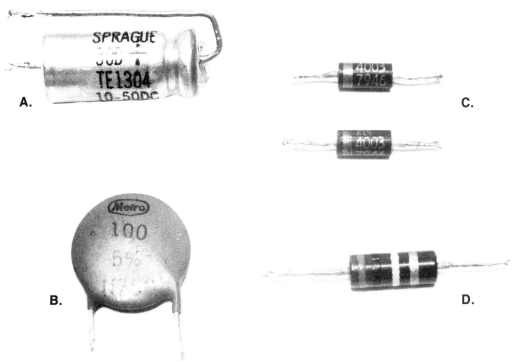

Fig. 3-19. Some components that may be found in small appliances: (A) an electrolytic capacitor has a negative and a positive connection; (B) capacitor without polarity; (C) two diodes—The band on the end indicates the direction of current flow—(D) a resistor whose resistance is indicated by the color-coded bands.

Motors are able to operate because we can convert electrical energy into mechanical energy. This is possible because of the characteristic of magnetic fields, which causes like poles to repel and unlike poles to attract. (The magnetic fields develop from the current that flows in the wires).

When a wire with current flowing through it is placed across a magnetic field, the magnetic field tries to push the conductor back out of the field. For example, if a rectangular-shaped piece of wire is placed between the two poles of a magnet, not much happens (FIG. 3-20). If, however, a battery is connected to the wire causing current to flow, a small amount of torque will be developed because of the new magnetic field developed around the wire and the magnetic field of the magnet (FIG. 3-21). This combination of forces creates a torque called *motor action* that turns the armature in an electric motor.

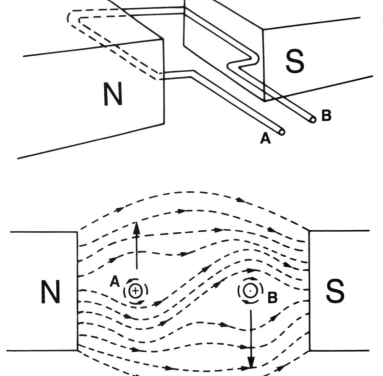

Fig. 3-20. Wire loop placed between the poles of a magnet.

Fig. 3-21. End view of the wire loop showing current flowing in **A** and coming out at **B**.

In our illustration, the wire loop will only rotate to a vertical position and then stop. To continue rotating, the current in the wire must change directions. This will cause the wire to develop a new magnetic field, but it will be in the opposite direction.

This change of direction can be accomplished by a simple switching device called a commutator. With the loop in one position, the current will flow from the negative contact through the left side of the loop and return back through the right side to the positive connection (FIG. 3-22). As the loop rotates through the vertical position, however, the contact that supplied the current to left side moves from the negative contact of the commutator to the positive contact. The right side of the loop is now touching the contact formerly used by the left side (FIG. 3-23). With the current and magnetic field in the wire loop reversed, rotation will continue. The operation of this simple motor will be jerky at best. A more functional motor with smoother torque can be made by adding more wire loops.

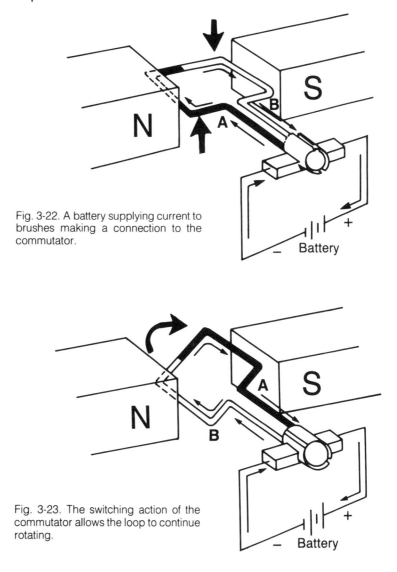

Fig. 3-22. A battery supplying current to brushes making a connection to the commutator.

Fig. 3-23. The switching action of the commutator allows the loop to continue rotating.

The core of the armature is usually made up of thin sheets of iron, which become part of the magnetic circuit (FIG. 3-24). Slots are located around the surface of the armature, providing a place to wind the coils. The armature winding is simply a series of coils wound on the iron core where the ends of the coils are connected to individual bars making up the commutator (FIG. 3-25). The copper bars in the commutator are positioned on insulated materials around the motor shaft (FIG. 3-26). These bars are also insulated from each other. The ends of the wires of the coils are next soldered to the copper bars, completing the armature's winding. As the armature turns, brushes are used to complete the electrical connection between the source and the armature winding.

The armature is positioned inside the iron frame because the frame is needed to complete the magnetic circuit. When voltage is applied to the brushes, the armature, being the only part of the motor free to rotate, turns slightly and tries to balance the magnetic fields. Before the magnetic fields become equal, however, that coil in the winding is disconnected by the switching action of the commutator, and another coil is rotated in its place, creating another unequal magnetic field. This sequence is repeated and the armature keeps rotating until the current stops flowing.

When this motor fails to operate, you first should check the continuity with an ohm meter. Simply connect the meter leads across the plug on the cord and turn the appliance switch on. On the R x 1 scale, the meter will just read a few ohms, indicating good connections. A reading of several thousand ohms usually indicates poor connections between the brushes and the commutator. If the meter fails to read at all, there is an open circuit, indicating a break in the cord, the coils, or the brushes. Sometimes, however, if a capacitor is in the circuit the meter will indicate an open circuit, but if the meter leads are reversed, the meter will briefly indicate continuity before it moves to the open reading.

Brushes are the most common cause of problems for these motors. The brushes are made of a carbon compound, and are mounted spring-loaded inside a brush holder. The brush should fit snugly in the holder, but must always be free to slide in and out. This action allows the spring to press the brush against the commutator, making the electrical connection. The commutator, as with any electrical contact, should be smooth and shiny where the brushes touch. Eventually the brushes will wear a groove all the way around the commutator, but the commutator still will be okay.

You can polish commutators with fine sandpaper. Do not use emery cloth because its metal grit will short between the copper bars.

You can make a continuity check with the meter on the high range, one lead connected to the commutator, and the other lead is connected to the core. The meter should read completely open. Next with the meter switched to the R x 1 scale, check the resistance between each bar of the commutator. They should all read about the same. Any drastic deviation in the meter reading probably indicates a defective coil. In most cases, the armature will need to be rewound or replaced.

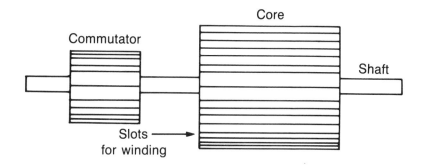

Fig. 3-24. An armature core without winding.

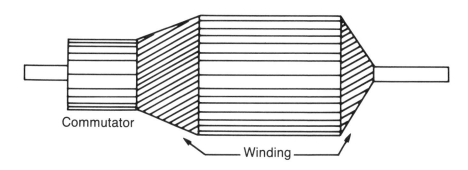

Fig. 3-25. An armature core with winding.

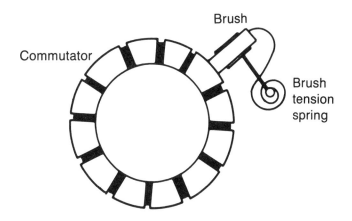

Fig. 3-26. End view of a commutator showing the brush connection.

BEARINGS

About the only other trouble spot in motors is the bearings, which usually consist of a simple sleeve or a brass ball with a hole in it. Some bearings have felt oil wicks for lubrication. Lint and debris will accumulate inside a motor and, after several years of buildup between the armature and the frame, will cause the motor to be overworked.

The solution to this problem is to take the motor apart and clean out the area between the armature and the frame, check the bearings for binding, make sure the brushes are free, and unplug any ventilating holes. A small soft paintbrush and an old toothbrush work very well. Avoid using solvents or cleaning fluids. They might dissolve the insulation around the windings. A thorough cleaning is usually not necessary. Just try to make sure that nothing is binding and the armature is free to rotate.

4
CHAPTER

Appliances

BAG SEALER

This rugged appliance is very useful for packaging seasonal fruits and vegetables for the freezer or simply putting up leftovers. It basically consists of a wire heating element controlled by a switch that is activated when the lid is closed. The transformer supplies power to the heating element and is connected to a line cord.

The most common problem with this appliance is caused by a faulty or damaged line cord. The only other trouble spots would be a defective switch or heating element, or a burned-out transformer. When a transformer burns out, a strong odor of burned varnish will be quite noticeable.

Fig. 4-1. Bag sealer.

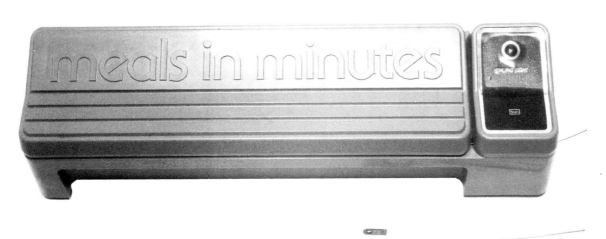

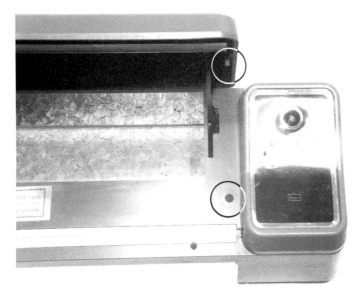

Fig. 4-2 (*left*) The switch mounted in the base is activated by a pin in the lid.

Fig. 4-3. (*below left*) A strip of fiberglass tape covers the heating element.

Fig. 4-4. (*bottom*) To get inside, remove the five Phillips screws from the bottom plate and separate the plate from the top cover.

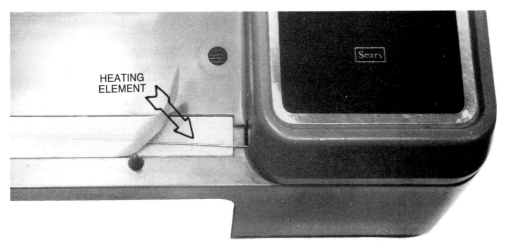

HEATING
ELEMENT

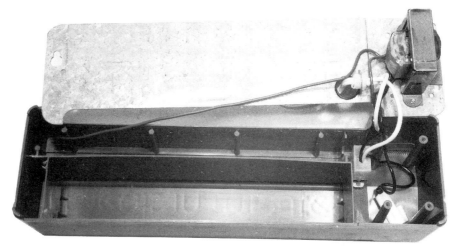

Fig. 4-5. (*above*) Then lift the plate containing the transformer from the top cover. Inspect the wiring going to the transformer switch and indicator lamp, as well as the connections to the heater.

Fig. 4-6. Check the transformer for any overheating, indicated by charred paper around the winding or a very strong odor.

Fig. 4-7. The terminal lead to one side of the heating element. A spring is used to maintain tension on the wire element.

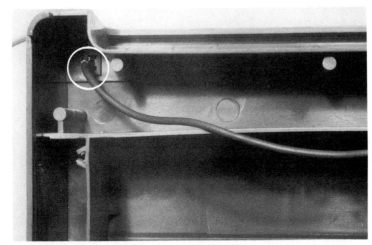

Fig. 4-8. The other end of the element is connected by a lug mounted on a wire.

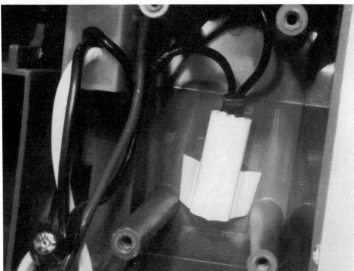

Fig. 4-9. Bottom view of the power indicator lamp.

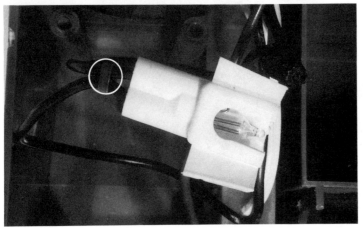

Fig. 4-10. The indicator light is held in place by its notched housing. A metal clamp holds the wires that keep the lamp positioned in the housing. Simply press the housing from the top and the indicator light pops free.

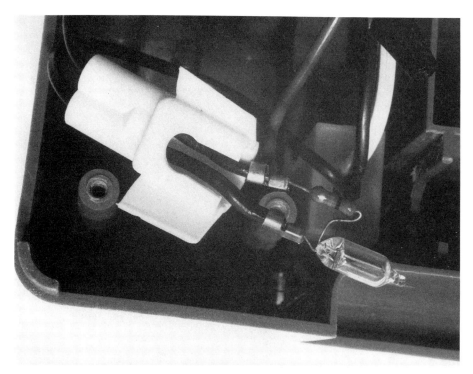

Fig. 4-11. Remove the clamp from the two wires at the base, then push the wires through to expose the lamp and a small resistor.

Fig. 4-12. The cover over the switch terminals.

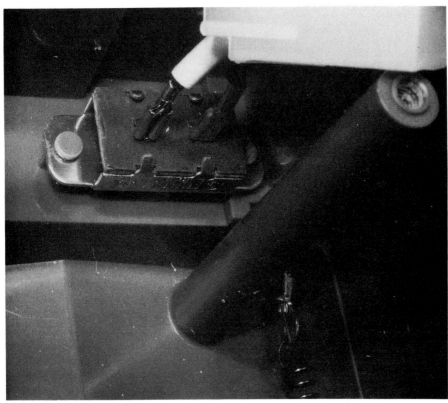

Fig. 4-13. Pry off the switch cover and inspect the terminal. If you need to replace the switch, you will need to drill out the switch mounts and use screws to install the new switch.

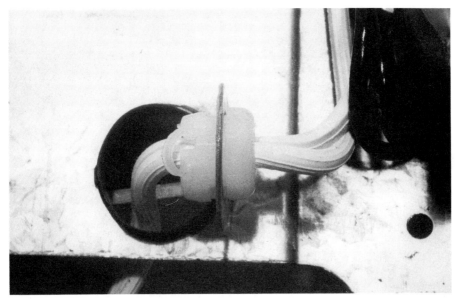

Fig. 4-14. Strain relief for the line cord.

BLADELESS GRASS TRIMMER

The bladeless grass trimmer is a very useful lawn care tool that should provide years of service with very little maintenance. Basically, it is nothing more than an electric motor spinning a spool of monofilament line.

The line cord enters the handle that contains a trigger-type switch. From the switch, a wire runs down the inside part of a tube to a motor housing. There, the wires are connected to the motor, which turns the spool assembly.

Probably the most troublesome part about the tool will be replacing the line since cement sidewalks and foundations tend to make short work of the cutting line. You must use care to cut only with the tip of the nylon line. The whirling action of the line will pick up dust particles and debris, and sling objects with enough speed to cause accidents. It makes good sense to wear safety goggles while operating this trimmer. Also avoid wearing open-toed or canvas shoes.

The only other source of problems would be a faulty cord or switch or the motor itself.

Fig. 5-1. Bladeless grass trimmer.

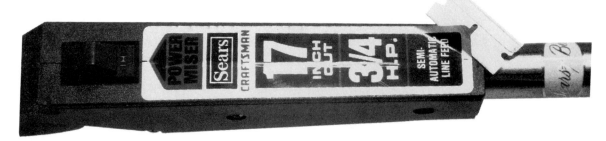

Fig. 5-2. To check out the switch and its connections, you will need to separate the two halves. Use a single-edged razor blade to pry up one corner of the decal, then gently pull the decal off, at least on one side.

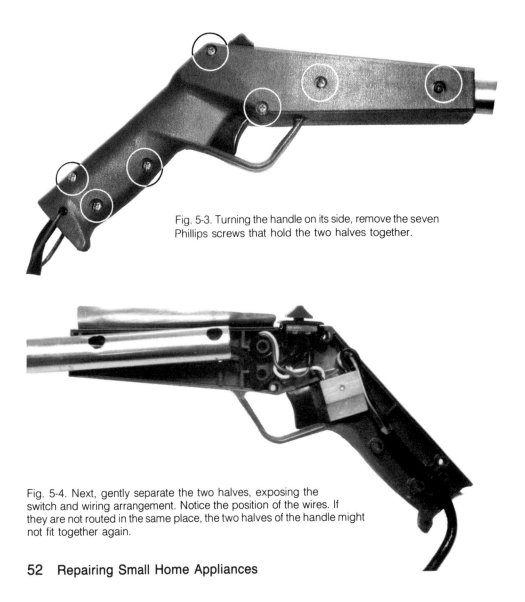

Fig. 5-3. Turning the handle on its side, remove the seven Phillips screws that hold the two halves together.

Fig. 5-4. Next, gently separate the two halves, exposing the switch and wiring arrangement. Notice the position of the wires. If they are not routed in the same place, the two halves of the handle might not fit together again.

Fig. 5-5. (*above*) To remove the trigger switch, simply insert a small jeweler's screwdriver or a paper clip in alongside the wire. Then pull the wire free. Be sure to label all wires to ensure proper reassembly.

Fig. 5-6. To get inside the lower housing, use the razor blade to peel up one-half of the decal.

Fig. 5-7. Next, remove the seven Phillips screws holding the two halves together, and gently separate the two halves of the housing.

Fig. 5-8. Notice how the motor fits in the housing. It must go back the same way. Lift out the motor for inspection or disassembly. The motor has a polarity, where one wire goes to the negative side and the other goes to the positive side. If the wires are swapped during reassembly, the motor will turn backward.

Fig. 5-9. Wire lug connected to brush assembly.

Fig. 5-10. Remove the spade connection and gently pry out the brush holder.

Fig. 5-11. For further disassembly, remove the hub assembly, or *spool cover*, and then the spool. A cotter key keeps the cover in place over the spool assembly.

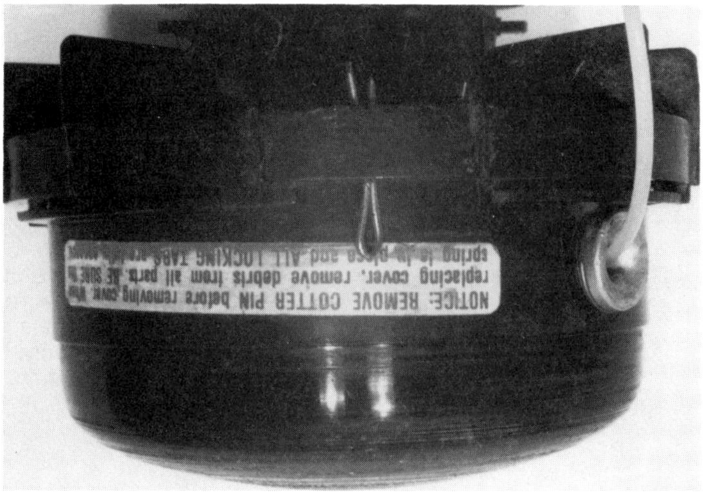

Fig. 5-12. The line spool is marked "TOP" and has an arrow indicating the direction of the line cord.

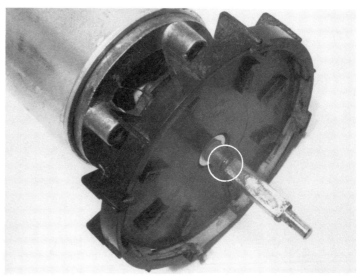

Fig. 5-13. Remove the small retaining ring from the shaft, then slide the top of the housing off the shaft.

Fig. 5-14. Two Phillips screws hold the motor housing together. This particular motor has strong permanent magnets mounted inside the housing. As a result, even after the two screws are removed, it will still take some effort to remove the armature.

Fig. 5-15. Armature after the housing and brushes have been removed.

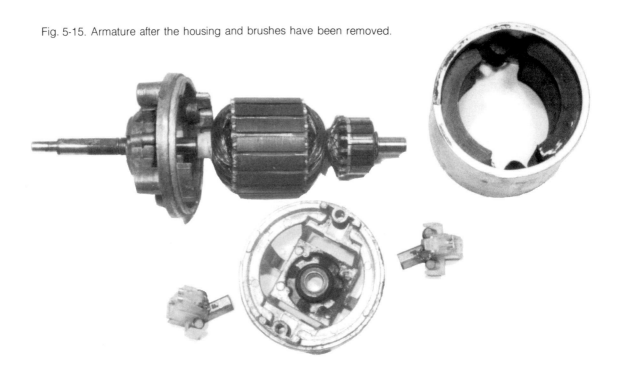

BLENDER

A blender can be thought of as a high-speed mixer, where knives mounted in the bottom of a glass or plastic container spin at high speeds and chop food into a very fine pulp.

The base of the blender houses the motor and a switch with several speed selections. On top of the base, a coupling is connected to the shaft of the motor. This coupling in turn fits into the coupling on the bottom of the food container. The coupling on the food container is attached to a shaft containing a set of sharp knives.

Fig. 6-1. Blender.

These blenders use speed to do the work and are not geared for power. Consequently, one of the most common abuses that leads to breakdown is attempting to grind or chop up heavy food products. Probably the most common malfunction is caused by allowing residue to build up around the shaft of the cutters. Eventually this will cause the bearing to seize, not allowing the shaft to rotate. This problem can be eliminated, however, by simply cleaning the food container immediately after using.

With any electric motor, when the start switch is pushed and the motor hums but doesn't turn, shut it off immediately. The motor might run, but will sound like it is laboring and may even start to smell. Again, shut it off immediately and determine why it is binding. The best preventive maintenance is to avoid heavy loads and clean the appliance after each use.

Fig. 6-2. Remove the four screws recessed inside the feet.

Fig. 6-3. Next, remove the retaining nut that secures the fan to the motor shaft.

Fig. 6-4. If the coupling is to be removed, grip the fan from the bottom and turn the coupling with pliers. For worn couplings, tap clockwise with a blunt object. If the coupling fails to turn, continue to disassemble the appliance until you have better access to the coupling and are able to grip the armature itself.

Fig. 6-5. The threaded end of the motor shaft after the coupling has been removed.

Fig. 6-6. A metal clip holds the brush assemblies in place.

Fig. 6-7. Remove the armature for inspection.

Fig. 6-8. The armature showing normal wear on the commutator.

Fig. 6-9. Take out the two retaining screws to remove the other half of the motor, or stator, assembly, and to reveal the shaft bearing and felt washer.

Fig. 6-10. Remove the two screws from the plate that keeps the bearing in place.

Fig. 6-11. Remove the bearing and felt ring from the housing.

Fig. 6-12. Separate the two halves of the housing and inspect all the internal wiring.

Fig. 6-13. Label the wires connected to the switch terminals before you disconnect them.

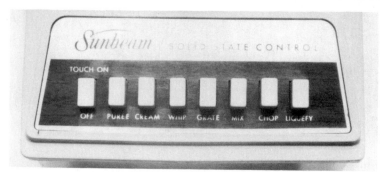

Fig. 6-14. The appliance can be disassembled completely, except for removal of the switches. Often the mounting screws are hidden underneath the label, which is usually destroyed when it is removed. Fortunately, the switches seldom need to be replaced.

Fig. 6-15. Remove the two screws at the top of the appliance, that hold the ring around the coupling area in place.

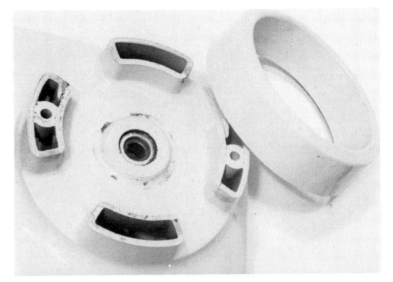

Fig. 6-16. The top of the appliance with the ring removed.

Fig. 6-17. When you reassemble the appliance, put the brushes in last, so the housing can be slid over the end of the armature. If you put the brushes in first, they will be in the way.

CAN OPENER

Electric can openers have been around for many years and tend to differ only slightly from one manufacturer to another. Basically, it is a device whereby a can is positioned between a gear and a cutting wheel, then a lever is pressed, forcing the cutting wheel into the top of the can. At this point a switch starts an electric motor, which turns a couple of drive gears on a shaft connected to a smaller gear, which turns the can. As the can turns, the cutting wheel cuts cleanly through the inside corner of the top of the can.

These appliances perform faithfully without any maintenance for years. You must keep the cutting wheel and gear clean, however, or the cutting wheel will not cut all the way around the lid. An old toothbrush and some soapy water will usually do the job. If not, you can remove the gear and wheel for cleaning. Just don't immerse the appliance in water.

Fig. 7-1. Can opener.

After many hours of use, the gears might become worn and cause a problem. The only other malfunction with this appliance is if the motor does not start. In this case, the trouble will be with the cord, the switch, or the motor itself.

Fig. 7-2. To remove the wheel cutter, simply remove the retaining screw with a standard screwdriver.

Fig. 7-3. The can opener with the cutting wheel removed and the cutting gear still attached.

Fig. 7-4. Before further disassembly, place a strip of tape across the switch button to keep it in place after the appliance comes apart.

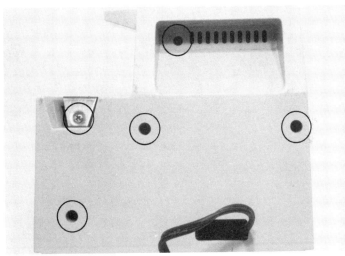

Fig. 7-5. Next, remove the five Phillips screws from the back of the unit, including the one holding the cover over the knife sharpener.

Fig. 7-6. Remove the top and front cover, exposing the grinding wheel.

Fig. 7-7. Then remove the remaining cover containing the motor assembly.

Fig. 7-8. You can disassemble the motor further by removing two screws.

Fig. 7-9. The motor disassembled. If the motor is bad,
you probably should replace the appliance.

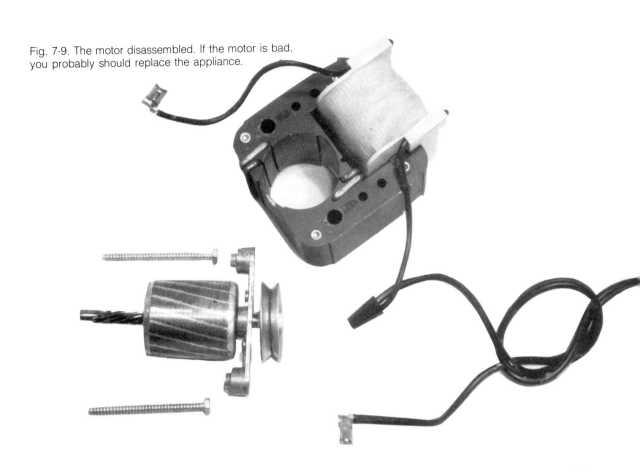

Fig. 7-10. The cutting gear is threaded on a shaft.

Fig. 7-11. To remove the cutting gear, hold the main gear from the back and remove the cutting gear with pliers. A 1/4-inch wrench extension will help hold the main gear while you are removing the cutting gear.

Fig. 7-12. The appliance with the main and cutting gears removed.

Fig. 7-13. To get to the switch, remove these two screws and the switch cover.

Fig. 7-14. Inspect the switch contacts. Problems with the switch are indicated by excessive pitting and corrosion. Contacts should be bright and shiny.

Fig. 7-15. The switch lifted from its bracket. Check wire connectors for a snug fit to the switch.

COFFEE MAKER WITH TIMER

Coffee makers can be found in a variety of sizes and shapes, all attempting to brew the perfect cup of coffee. Inside, however, they have a number of things in common. They have a heating element, usually controlled by a thermostat of some sort, that allows the coffee to brew and then continues to keep it warm afterwards. Some models have a fixed thermostat and cannot be adjusted by the user. Other models are equipped with a variable thermostat providing more control over the strength of the coffee.

NOTE: Please read the Notices on the Copyright page at the front of this book.

Fig. 8-1. Coffee maker with timer.

A typical arrangement would be one in which a small amount of fresh water is heated, which causes it to move upward through a tube and then to drip down through the coffee. The cold water keeps the thermostat turned on until the heating element has brought all of the water up to a temperature hot enough to cause it to percolate through the tube. When the water reaches the proper temperature, the thermostat turns off the heating element. As the coffee starts to cool, however, the thermostat closes, allowing the element to heat up again and keep the coffee warm. Some coffee makers have a separate warming element that comes on when the thermostat opens.

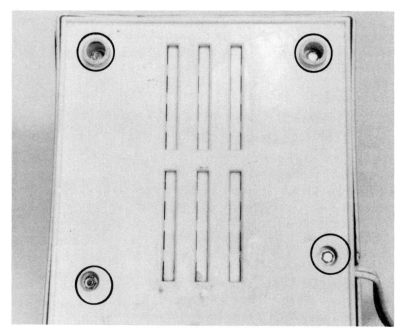

Fig. 8-2. Remove the four retaining screws from the bottom.

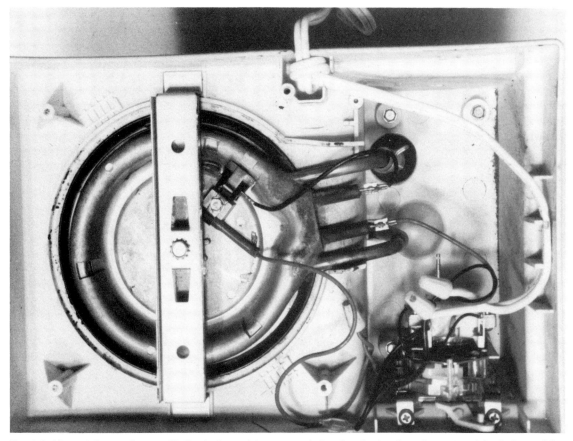

Fig. 8-3. View of the appliance with the bottom plate removed showing the heating element and the bottom of the clockworks.

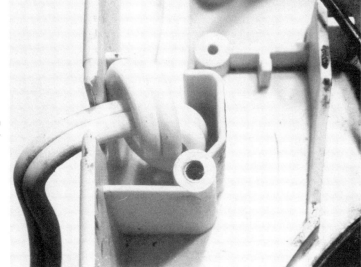

Fig. 8-4. A strain relief knot keeps tension from being applied to the cord connections inside the appliance.

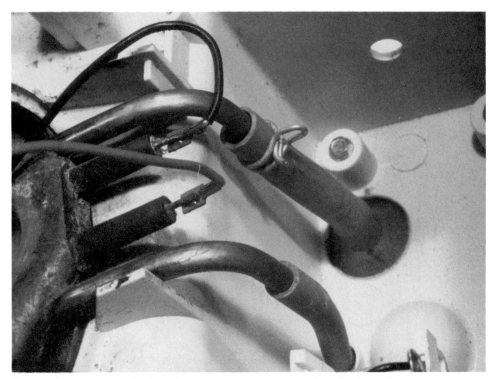

Fig. 8-5. To remove the heating element, remove the clamps from the flow tubes.

Fig. 8-6. Next remove the single bolt on the bracket that keeps the heating element assembly in place.

Fig. 8-7. The heating element assembly with thermostat.

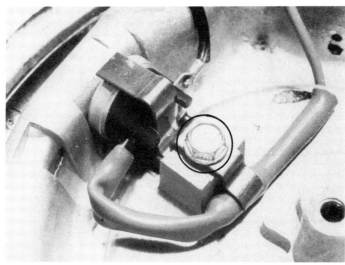

Fig. 8-8. Now remove the element along with the exposed thermostat. The thermostat is held in place by a single retaining screw.

Fig. 8-9. The numbers on top of the thermostat are important when you are purchasing a replacement.

Fig. 8-10. Remove the four Phillips screws holding the top of the housing. Then remove the housing to reveal the drip dispersion assembly.

Fig. 8-11. (*below*) View of the appliance with the top cover removed.

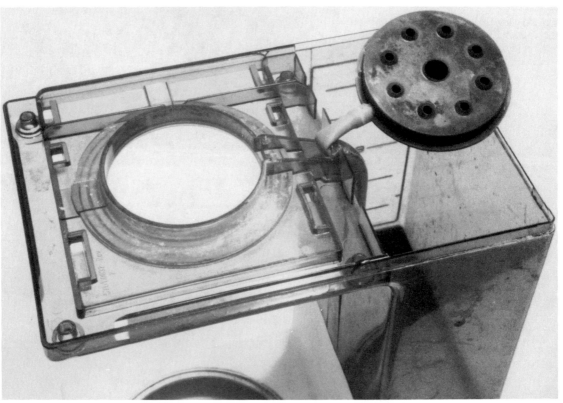

Fig. 8-12. Use a screwdriver to gently pry off the cover for the clock assembly.

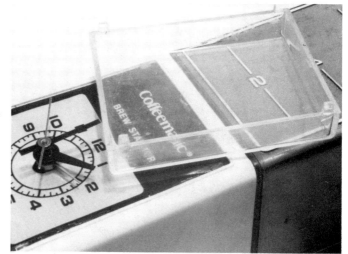

Fig. 8-13. The hands of the clock have an expansion gap in the center, which enables you to carefully press them on and off.

Fig. 8-14. Each hand has a different size hub so you can place the hands on the proper shaft in the proper order.

Fig. 8-15. Take off the two Phillips screws and the clamps to remove the clock assembly.

Fig. 8-16. The coffee maker with the clockworks removed.

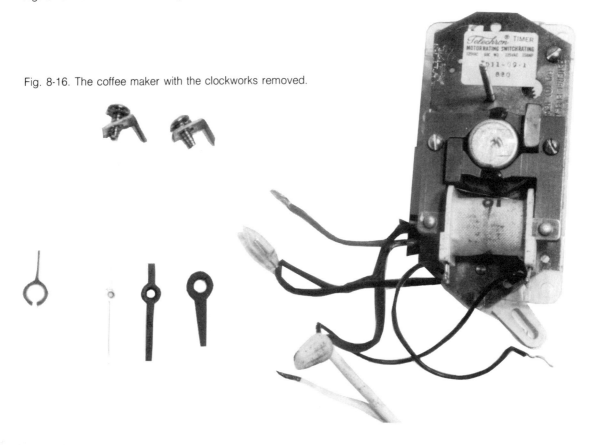

DEEP FRYER

The deep fryer, or french fryer, is a simple appliance similar to a skillet or griddle. It basically consists of a line cord connected to a heating element, with a thermostat controlling the temperature. Often there is a neon lamp connected across the thermostat. When the heating element reaches a preset temperature sensed by the thermostat, the thermostat opens. The lamp lights, indicating the fryer is ready to use.

The simplicity of this appliance limits problems to a faulty line cord or thermostat, but occasionally the heating elements do burnout.

Fig. 9-1. Deep fryer.

Fig. 9-2. Remove the three Phillips screws in the bottom.

Fig. 9-3. Remove the two nuts holding the prongs for the plug connection.

Fig. 9-4. The heating element and the thermostat are now open for inspection.

Fig. 9-5. To remove the thermostat, disconnect one terminal lug and remove the Phillips screw holding the thermostat in place.

DRILL

The electric drill is probably one of the most widely owned power tools. It consists of a line cord connected to a motor controlled by a trigger switch. The motor drives a set of reduction gears connected to a shaft. The shaft is then threaded into an adjustable chuck that holds the bits.

A common problem is a faulty power cord. This problem is often caused by carrying the drill by the cord, or by pulling on the cord to unplug the drill, instead of pulling the plug itself. Other problems can occur because the motor has been overworked. This problem occurs from applying too much pressure, or bearing down on the drill and not allowing it to work at its own pace. Further abuse of the motor can be caused by using a larger bit or blade than the drill was designed for. Continued overloading of the motor could burn out the armature.

If the drill fails to operate at all check the cord and the switch. If they are okay, take a look at the brushes and then the motor. If the motor hums but the drill will not turn or if it turns but is unusually noisy, the problem is probably in the gears. With a little care and using sharp bits, this handy tool will last for years.

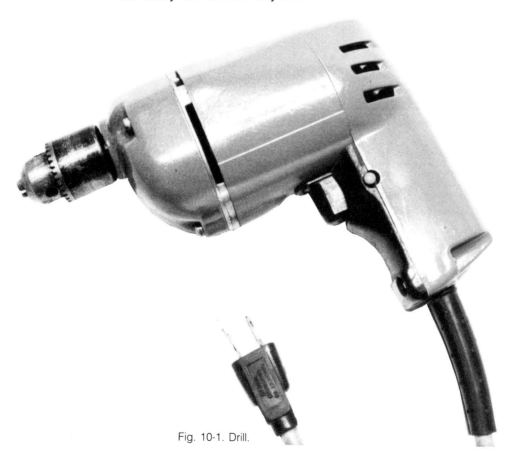

Fig. 10-1. Drill.

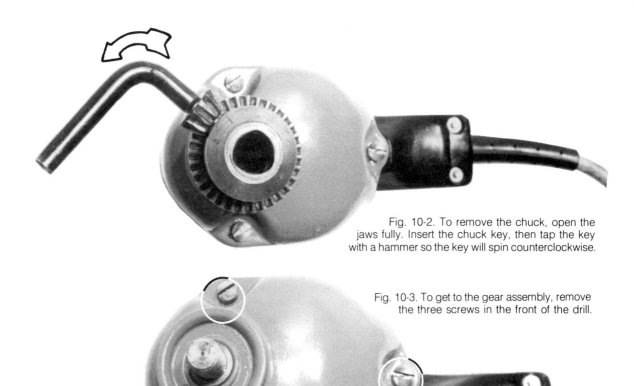

Fig. 10-2. To remove the chuck, open the jaws fully. Insert the chuck key, then tap the key with a hammer so the key will spin counterclockwise.

Fig. 10-3. To get to the gear assembly, remove the three screws in the front of the drill.

Fig. 10-4. Gear assembly.

Fig. 10-5. Remove the front housing and open to inspect the gears.

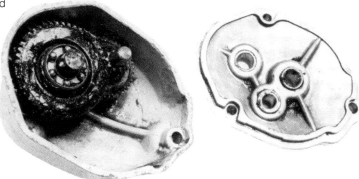

Fig. 10-6. To get to the switch and brushes, remove the four screws in the back of the handle.

Fig. 10-7. Remove the handle and inspect the internal wiring.

Fig. 10-8. Remove the brushes with the tip of a flat screwdriver.

Fig. 10-9. Wire clips make the electrical connection to the brushes.

Fig. 10-10. End view of the motor assembly. For further disassembly, remove the clamp connector to the brush holders.

Fig. 10-11. Next remove the fan shroud and armature (*shown*).

Fig. 10-12. Two screws are left holding the windings in place.

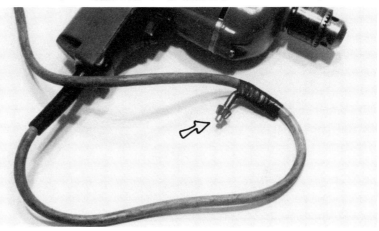

Fig. 10-13. The chuck key will always be handy if you tape it to the line cord about 2 feet down from the drill.

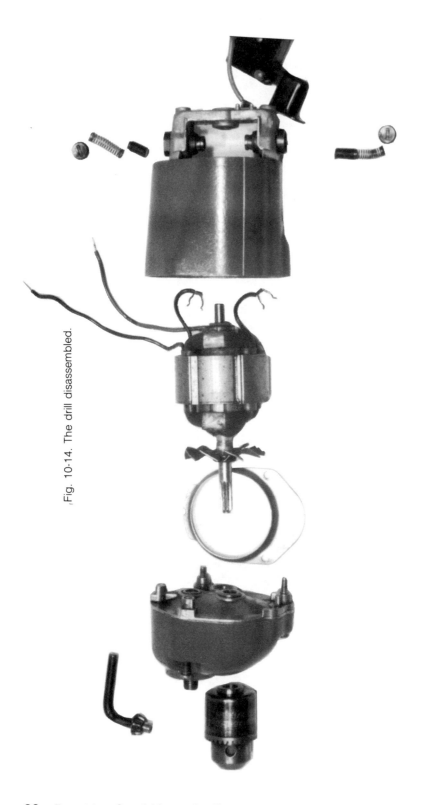

Fig. 10-14. The drill disassembled.

ELECTRIC KNIFE

An electric knife is a very worthwhile appliance to own, and problems generally occur after the blades have become dull and the knife is forced down, or sawed, to help the cutting action. You should guide, not push, an electric knife. Let it do the work.

Electric knives are equipped with two serrated blades that ride next to each other. The cutting action is produced when the motor rotates two cams, pushing one blade forward while pulling the other one back. As the motor continues to turn, the action is reversed and the first blade is pulled back, pushing the other one forward. This system works very well using only a guiding motion with the handle. Styrofoam and frozen foods take a heavy toll on the blades, however, so do not cut them with an electric knife.

Eventually, brushes could cause a problem, but by far the majority of problems are caused from dull blades or misaligned blades. The only other source of trouble would be the switch or a worn gear. Generally if these blades are kept clean and not abused, this handy appliance will be a great labor-saving device.

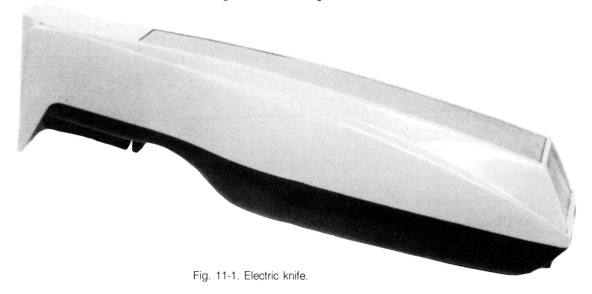

Fig. 11-1. Electric knife.

Fig. 11-2. (*above*) To disassemble this appliance, remove the four Phillips screws on the bottom.

Fig. 11-3. (*left*) Then remove the two small Phillips screws on the front.

Fig. 11-4. (*below*) Carefully separate the two halves. Next, remove the two screws just behind the fan.

Fig. 11-5. Lift the motor assembly out of its housing.

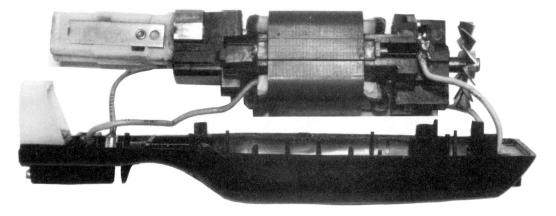

Fig. 11-6. Screw holding the switch terminal in place.

Fig. 11-7. To get to the switch contacts, gently pry the wire lug from its terminal and remove the retaining screw. Next remove the screw from the end of the switch button.

Fig. 11-8. Examine the contacts.

FAN, DESKTOP

A small personal fan, although relatively inexpensive, should not be discarded at the first sign of problems. These fans are not usually moved about much, so the line cord generally does not create a problem. The switches tend to be rather simple. Spraying the switches with the proper cleaner/lubricant tends to solve most of the problems.

The small motor inside, however, can be overloaded by lack of housekeeping or positioning the fan in such a way that would restrict the amount of air coming into the appliance. As with most appliances employing a motor that has very little torque, any increase on the load of the motor will greatly decrease the life of the appliance.

Fig. 12-1. Desktop fan.

Fig. 12-2. To disassemble the fan, remove the four recessed screws on the bottom and separate the two halves.

Fig. 12-3. Fan with the top cover removed.

Fig. 12-4. Fan control switch.

Fig. 12-5. To remove the switch, simply press the ends of the switch together and push toward the outside of the housing. The motor assembly is held in place by the two recessed nuts on the bottom.

FAN, OSCILLATING

Basically, an electric fan is an appliance, where blades are connected to the shaft of a motor, which is connected to a line cord. A selector switch controls the speed of the motor. Their only purpose is to move a column of air.

The small oscillating fan is the most common one found around households. These fans are mounted in such a manner where the motor can be set to swivel back and forth, changing the direction of the deflected air.

An efficient fan will move an appropriate amount of air, but by doing so, it is also moving a proportional amount of dust and lint. Eventually this dirt can clog the oscillating gears and build up on the blades themselves. If the blades are to perform, they must be kept clean and smooth. The extra buildup not only reduces the blades' efficiency, it increases the load on the motor. Additional accumulations of dust tend to clog the gears, producing an additional strain on the motor, eventually causing this worthwhile appliance to become an undesirable nuisance. Seldom does the switch or cord create a problem. A quality fan will run almost silently for years with only an occasional cleaning.

Fig. 13-1. Oscillating fan.

Fig. 13-2. Begin by prying open the three clips that hold the front half of the blade guard. You might need a screwdriver.

Fig. 13-3. A metal blade will probably have a set screw; however, this plastic blade is held in place by a large nut called the *spinner*. Remove the plastic nut.

Fig. 13-4. Remove the pin in the shaft, which locks the blades in place. Next, remove the remaining plastic nut and remove the back half of the guard.

Fig. 13-5. To get inside the back housing, remove the oscillating control knob. Some are held on by screws; others can just be pulled off.

Fig. 13-6. Remove the Phillips screw on the back of the motor housing.

Fig. 13-7. Remove the two Phillips screws on the front of the housing and take out the motor.

Fig. 13-8. If the fan refuses to turn and the continuity check indicated an open circuit, look for a blown fuse.

Fig. 13-9. Some motors have a fuse to protect them from motor overloads. This one is located in plastic tubing folded in next to the motor windings. They're often held in place by wraps of twine.

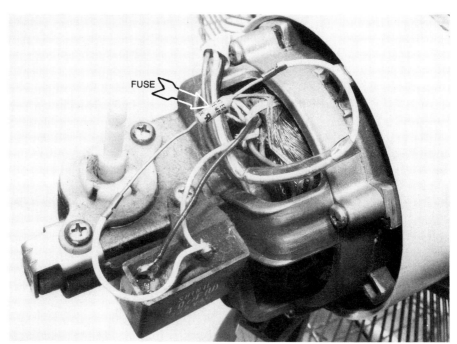

FUSE

Fig. 13-10. To check the fuse, carefully snip the twine and remove the fuse from the motor housing, being careful not to damage the insulated finish on the winding. Next unfold the wire from the motor housing and slide the tubing from the fuse. To test any fuse for continuity, disconnect one of the ends of the fuse before connecting the meter. Otherwise, instead of reading the value of the fuse, the meter might indicate the resistance of the circuit itself.

Fig. 13-11. If the fuse is bad, make sure the motor shafts spins freely and the oscillating gear is not jammed, then install a new fuse.

FOOD PROCESSOR

If a food processor fails to start, it is usually because the bowl is not locked in place. Blades on food processors are very sharp and can be dangerous. For this reason, these appliances are equipped with safety interlocks that prevent the motor from running if the bowl is not in place. Another safety switch turns the motor off if the blades become overloaded or jammed.

The best preventive maintenance is to keep the food processor clean, especially the blade area. The blade assembly must fit over the shaft smoothly. Any obstruction in this connection, causing an improper fit, will make the blades wobble. Troubles can occur from a defective switch or line cord, and motors do go bad, but you can avoid most problems by properly cleaning the food processor after each use.

Fig. 14-1. Food processor.

Fig. 14-2. Remove the two recessed screws and the two small Phillips screws on the bottom, which hold the bottom housing in place.

Fig. 14-3. Bottom of food processor with housing removed.

Fig. 14-4. To remove the switches, slide the indicator lamp from its housing. Next remove the two Phillips screws holding the switches in place. Notice the way the wires are routed along the side. Be sure to put them back in the same place when reassembling.

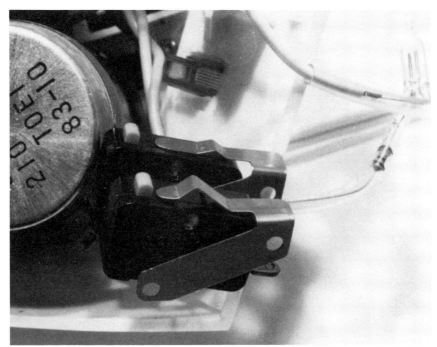

Fig. 14-5. To separate the two switches, remove the two Phillips screws and nuts from the switch bracket.

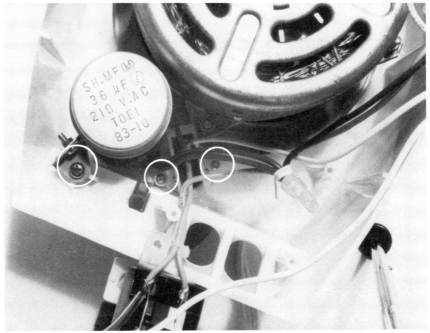

Fig. 14-6. Remove the one Phillips screw that holds the capacitor in place, then remove the two smaller Phillips screws holding the other indicator lamp in place, and lift out the rest of the electrical assembly.

Fig. 14-7. The capacitor and indicator lamp free from the housing.

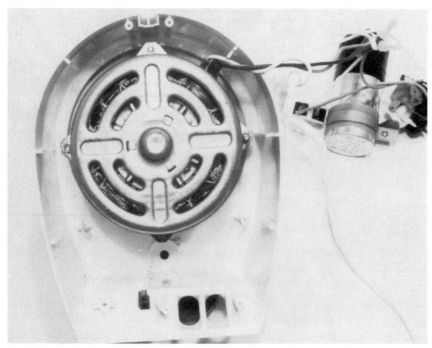

Fig. 14-8. The bottom view of the motor. Further dissasembly is probably unnecessary. If the motor is bad, you probably need a new food processor.

FOOD SLICER

Basically a food slicer is a power cord connected to a motor that turns a geared serrated circular blade. This handy appliance does an excellent job of slicing food, such as meats and cheeses. A knob is used to move a guide that varies the thickness of each slice.

Problems could come from a faulty cord or switch, but most complaints come from a dull blade. Bones, frozen food, and even aluminum foil can quickly dull the blade. As the blade becomes dull, excessive pressure is used to do the slicing. This pressure puts a strain on the motor and shortens the life of the gears. Excessive noise while operating usually indicates a gear problem. These problems can be avoided by keeping the blade sharp and not abusing it.

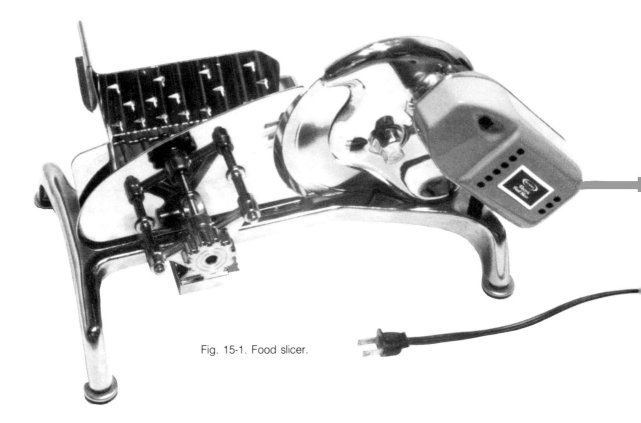

Fig. 15-1. Food slicer.

Fig. 15-2. Begin disassembly by loosening the retaining screw on the blade guard and removing the drive unit.

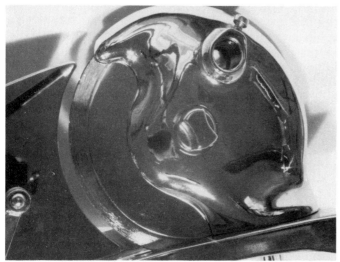

Fig. 15-3. Next remove the nut that holds the blade in place.

Fig. 15-4. Remove the smaller gear using a large screwdriver.

Fig. 15-5. Check the gear for missing or worn teeth.

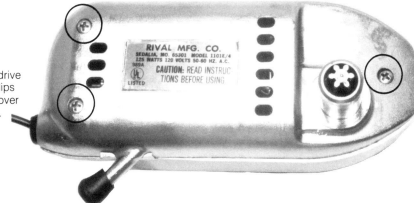

Fig. 15-6. To get inside the drive unit, remove the three Phillips screws on the back of the cover and separate the two halves.

Fig. 15-7. Remove the two Phillips screws that hold the switch in place.

Fig. 15-8. Notice the information marked on the side of the switch.

Food Slicer **109**

Fig. 15-9. To inspect the brushes, remove the two Phillips screws on the end, which hold the bearing in place. Next, remove the four Phillips screws alongside the motor. Finally, remove the two Phillips screws that hold the remaining bearing in place.

Fig. 15-10. After lifting the motor from its housing (see Fig. 15-12), slip out the drive gear.

Fig. 15-11. Check the gear for worn or missing teeth.

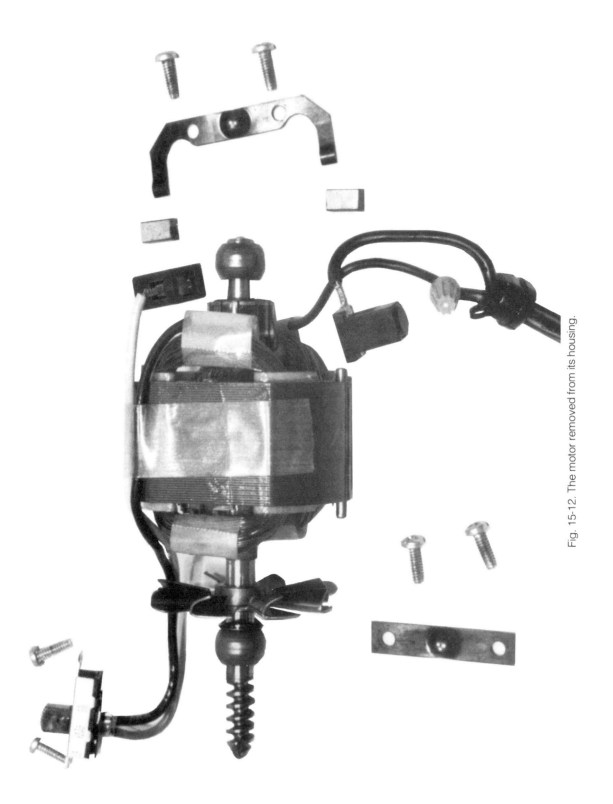

Fig. 15-12. The motor removed from its housing.

FOOT MASSAGER

This small appliance offers relief for tired feet and is helpful in relieving tension. The line cord is connected to a selector switch, which in turn is connected to a small motor. One position of the switch is connected to the motor, and the other is connected to a heating element. In this way the massager can be used alone or if desired, with warm water for a therapeutic foot bath. The appliance is normally not abused and is usually trouble free. Cords can become damaged, however, and switches can malfunction. This is a safe appliance, but you should exercise caution any time water is used around electricity. The foot massager has a heater between the foot pad. *Do not* remove the four small Phillips screws since the heater seal may be damaged and water might get to the element. This would definitely cause a severe shock.

Fig. 16-1. Foot massager.

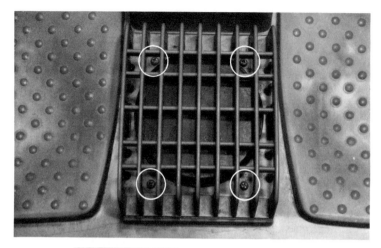

Fig. 16-2. The heating element is sealed and held in place by four small Phillips screws. Do not remove these screws.

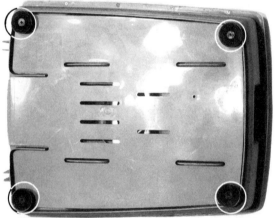

Fig. 16-3. To get inside, remove the four screws in the feet on the bottom.

Fig. 16-4. Remove the cover. You can now see the wiring going to the vibrator motor and the heating element.

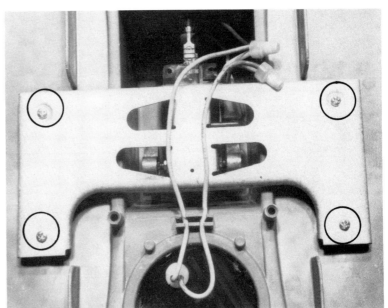

Fig. 16-5. To get to the motor, remove the four Phillips screws holding the motor bracket to the housing. To remove the motor, disconnect the wire lugs from their terminals on the motor.

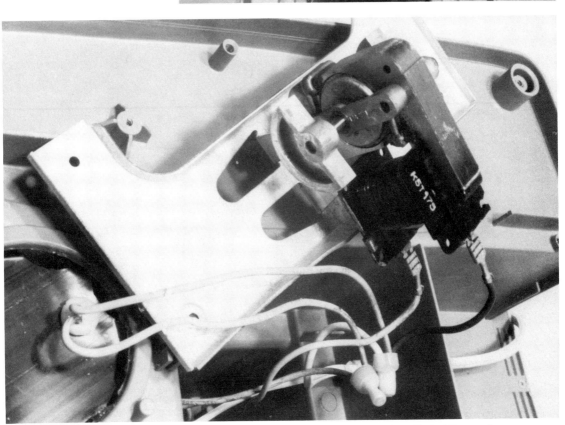

Fig. 16-6. The off-center weights on the motor shaft create the massaging effect of the appliance.

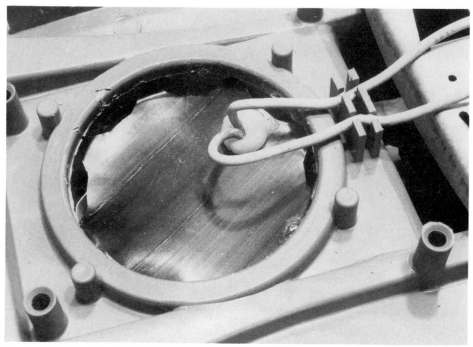

Fig. 16-7. The heating unit is sealed behind this cover. No repair is recommended. If the heater is bad, replace the appliance.

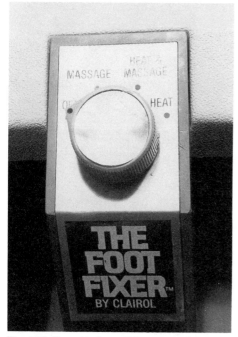

Fig. 16-8. To get to the switch, remove the cover on the control knob.

Fig. 16-9. Carefully peel off the metal plate on top of the knob. Next remove the countersunk Phillips screw.

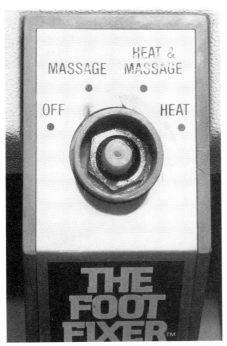

Fig. 16-10. A nut secures the switch to the housing. Remove the nut and lift out the switch from the bottom.

Fig. 16-11. On the back of the switch, each terminal is numbered. Label the wires before you disconnect them from the switch.

Fig. 16-12. Pry apart the switch to inspect the contact. Be careful when you separate the two halves of the switch, however, because the pieces could fly all over.

Foot Massager 117

GARBAGE DISPOSAL

Garbage disposals tend to receive heavy use around most households, but they will last many years if not abused. It consists of a motor turning a flywheel containing moveable weights inside a shredder ring. The motor usually receives its power from a line cord plugged into a receptacle underneath the sink. Power to the receptacle is controlled by a switch mounted on the wall next to the sink.

The most common complaint with this appliance comes when the disposal jams. If the switch is turned on and the motor just hums but doesn't run, it probably means the flywheel is jammed. Immediately turn the switch off. Use a wooden plunger handle or broom handle in a rotary

Fig. 17-1. Garbage disposal.

fashion to free the flywheel. Use tongs to fish out any silverware that might have fallen in. Then try the switch again. If you were successful in freeing the flywheel and the motor turns, drop in a few ice cubes to help free any remaining restrictions.

If the motor doesn't hum at all and nothing happens when the switch is turned on, it probably means that the motor's overload protection was brought into play. Some disposals eventually reset themselves; this one, however, has a reset button on the bottom of the motor that must be pressed. In some cases, the motor might have to cool for 10 or 15 minutes before the button can be reset. Because these motors have overload protection they seldom fail, but if the motor does burn out, the disposal must be replaced.

You can avoid most problems by keeping glass, paper, dishrags, and silverware out of the appliance. Don't pack the garbage, but feed it to the disposal along with plenty of cold water. When it is finished grinding, continue to run cold water for a few seconds.

If you cannot free the flywheel, you will need to drop the unit from the sink and open it up. Begin by disconnecting the power. Usually this means unplugging the unit from the receptacle underneath the sink. If this is not possible, trip the circuit breaker in the main panel, then disconnect the wires feeding into the bottom of the motor. Then work according to the following instructions, given with the photographs.

A garbage disposal is usually not difficult to work on. Getting to one, however, can be very trying because of the limited working space. It is very important to follow the owner's manual and to consider the kind of garbage that your disposal can handle.

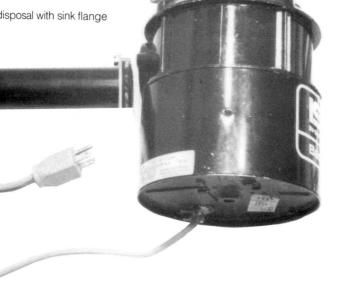

Fig. 17-2. Garbage disposal with sink flange disassembled.

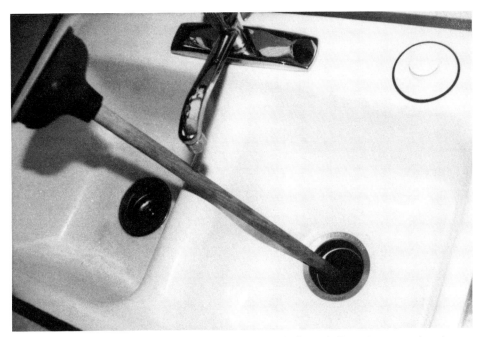

Fig. 17-3. Use a wooden handle to try to free a jammed disposal. Do not use your hand.

Fig. 17-4. Usually a single screw holds an access plate over the opening containing the wire connections. Unscrew it, then disconnect the drainpipe from the drain. If the trap must be removed, have a drip pan and a few paper towels handy. Next disconnect the dishwasher connection (usually a hose clamp located on the fitting above the drain).

Fig. 17-5. Now loosen the three screws located in the support flange, but don't take them out. Then, with the drains disconnected, rotate the supporting ring slightly, freeing the unit from the bottom of the sink.

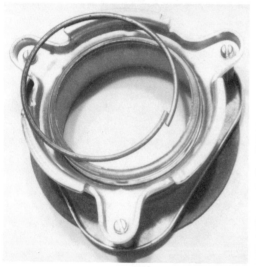

Fig. 17-6. (*above left*) Remove the retaining ring holding the sink flange and supporting ring in place.

Fig. 17-7. (*above right*) The rubber drain cover snaps over the lip on the top of the housing.

Fig. 17-8. Remove the two screws that hold the flange connecting the drainpipe to the housing.

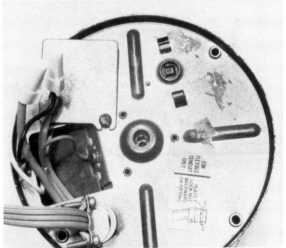

Fig. 17-9. (*above left*) The top of the unit with the drain cover removed. A little lubrication on the lip will help when installing a new rubber cover.

Fig. 17-10. (*above right*) Bottom view of the motor, showing the reset button and four screws holding the motor housing together.

Fig. 17-11. (*center*) The wire connection is under the access plate on the bottom of the motor.

Fig. 17-12. (*right*) To get to the flywheel, remove the four long screws from the bottom of the motor housing. Then separate the upper third of the housing from the rest of the assembly. Inspect the shredder ring. Remove the nut in the center, which holds the flywheel to the shaft and inspect the flywheel.

GRIDDLE

Most of today's electric griddles have sealed heating elements, allowing the griddle to be immersed in water or run through a dishwasher. If the element on such a unit is bad, however, it cannot be replaced. Fortunately the heating element seldom causes problems.

Problems are confined to the line cord or the temperature control. The probe on the end of the control is a heat-sensing probe. This probe, located between the two electrical contacts, senses the temperature for the thermostat. As the cooking surface heats, the heat travels along the probe and up to the thermostat. The thermostat is adjustable and controlled by a knob on the control unit. Never immerse these control units in water and, as with any appliance using a detachable control unit, always connect the heat control to the appliance first and then plug the cord into the wall outlet. To disconnect, turn the control off then remove the plug from the wall outlet.

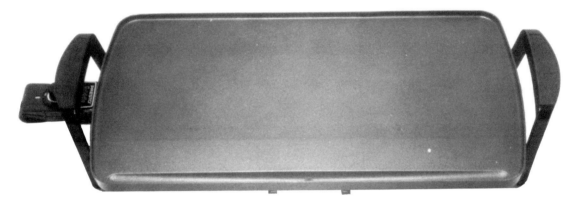

Fig. 18-1. Griddle.

Fig. 18-2. Bottom view of griddle, showing the sealed heating element.

Most griddles are coated with a nonsticking surface and are best cleaned with warm, soapy water, then rinsed and dried. Never use steel wool or an abrasive kitchen cleaner.

Fig. 18-3. If this or any appliance trips a circuit breaker, first check from the plug of the appliance for a short. Then check the element to the appliance. If the cord was the problem, you can replace it. If the element was shorted, you need a new griddle.

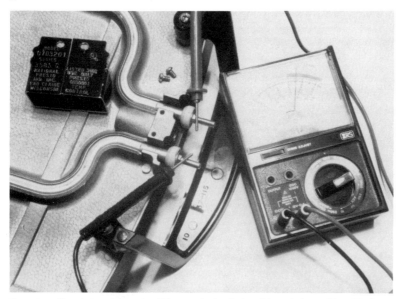

Fig. 18-4. Check the element itself for continuity. It should read about 20 to 30 ohms.

Fig. 18-5. To get inside the control, remove the four Phillips screws on the back and gently separate the two halves.

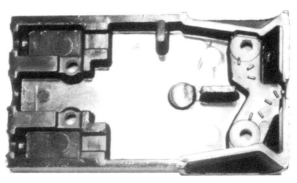

Fig. 18-6. The inside of the control unit.

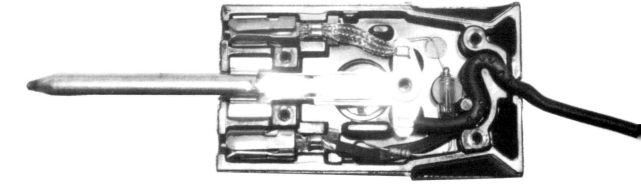

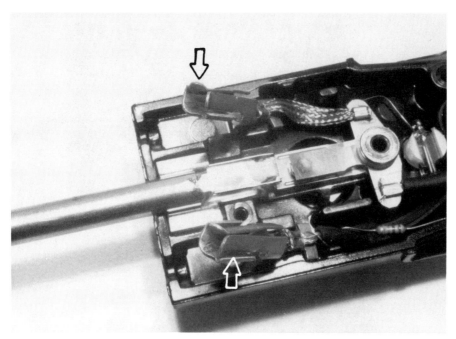

Fig. 18-7. Gently pry out the pin terminals and inspect them.

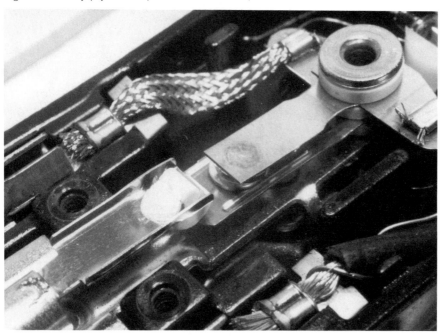

Fig. 18-8. Always take time to check the contacts of the thermostat for arcing or pitting.

HAIR DRYER, HAND-HELD

Today's hair styles make the hand-held hair dryer one of the most used appliances around the home. It consists of a motor-driven impeller that blows air over a heating element. The speed of the motor and the temperature of the heating element are controlled by a switch or a number of switches positioned in the handle. Preventive maintenance on this appliance is limited to keeping hair and lint from around the impeller. Faulty cords can be replaced, but the popularity of this appliance has made them relatively inexpensive, so if the motor or heating element becomes defective, it is usually more practical to replace the dryer.

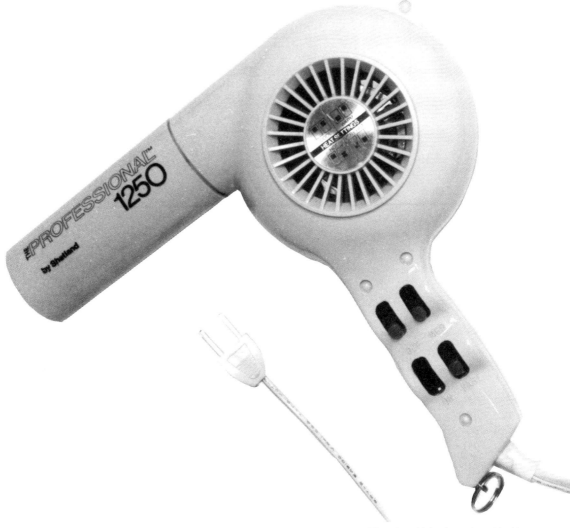

Fig. 19-1. Hair dryer, hand-held.

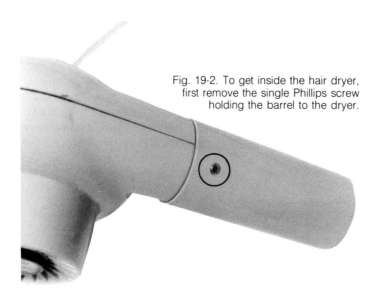

Fig. 19-2. To get inside the hair dryer, first remove the single Phillips screw holding the barrel to the dryer.

Fig. 19-3. Next gently work and twist the barrel free of the dryer. Also remove the insulator from the heating element.

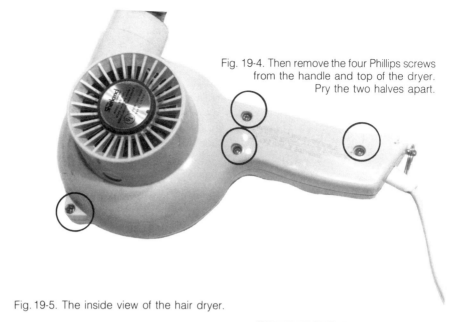

Fig. 19-4. Then remove the four Phillips screws from the handle and top of the dryer. Pry the two halves apart.

Fig. 19-5. The inside view of the hair dryer.

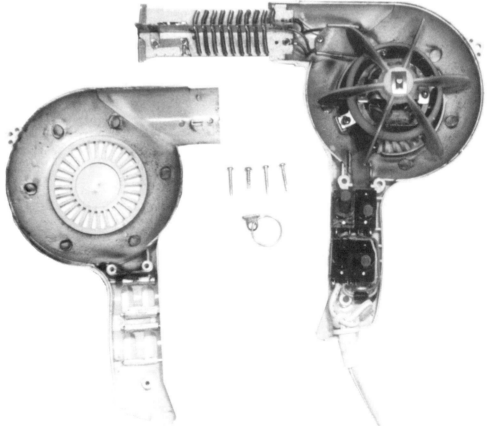

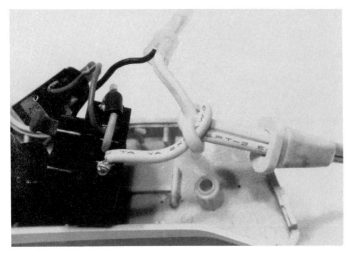

Fig. 19-6. The line cord shows the Underwriters' knot. Inspect the cord.

Fig. 19-7. Four switches control the operation of this dryer. Remove and replace them if necessary.

Fig. 19-8. To remove the motor and fan assembly, remove the two Phillips screws on the side of the motor bracket.

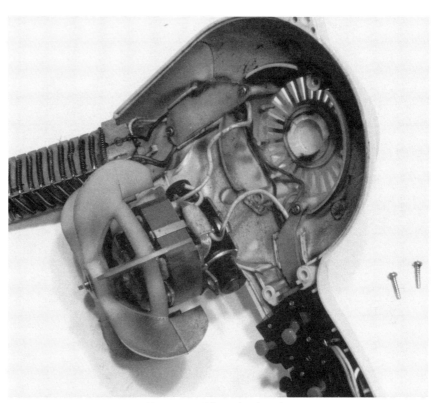

Fig. 19-9. The motor assembly removed from the housing.

Fig. 19-10. Inspect the brushes and the commutator for wear.

HAIR DRYER WITH BONNET

Hair dryers of this type tend to receive moderate use, which extends their life considerably. The base contains a motor, which turns a fan or impeller, which moves a column of air over a heating element. This operation is controlled by a selector switch also mounted on the base. Positions of the switch dictate air flow, as well as levels of temperature. The air is then forced from the base through a hose or ductwork up into the bonnet.

Problems from this appliance usually come from a faulty line cord or switch. Occasionally, however, the heating element burns out, and the impeller sometimes collects enough lint or debris that it will not turn. It doesn't happen often, but if the motor does burn out, consider purchasing another hair dryer. Preventive maintenance for this appliance is nothing more than not abusing the power cord and keeping air intakes free of lint and hair.

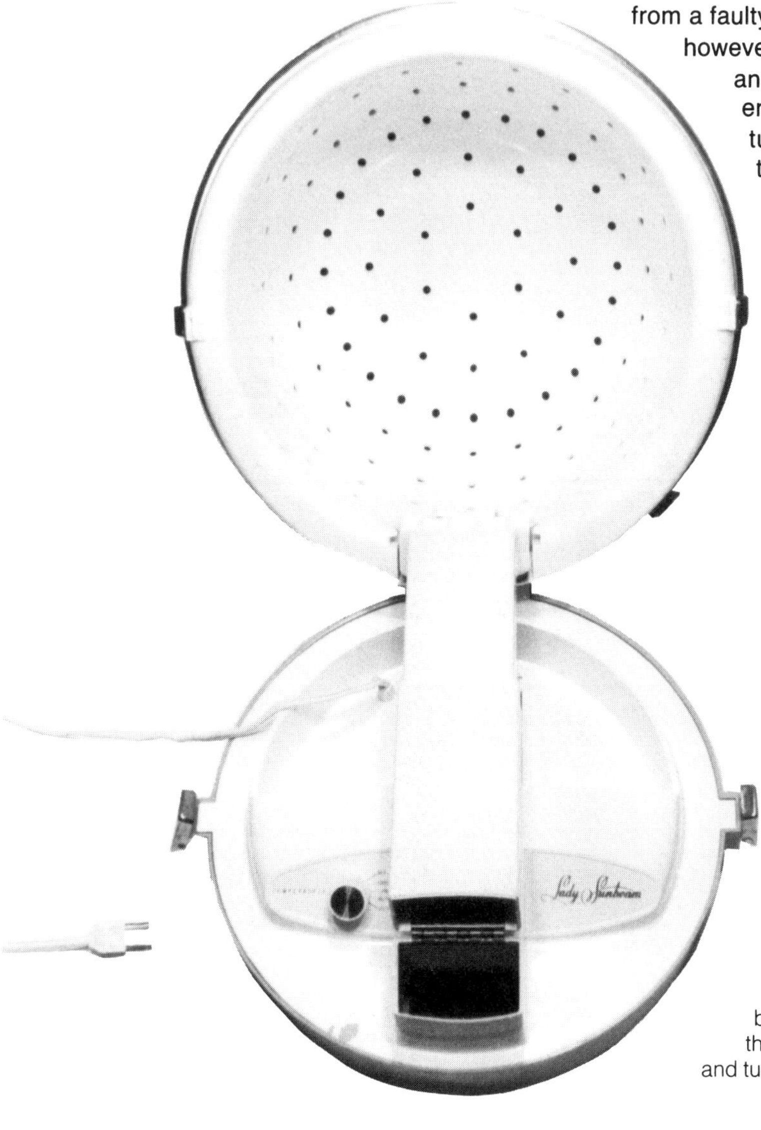

Fig. 20-1. Hair dryer with bonnet. Use a vegetable strainer or plastic bowl as a base when you disassemble the hair dryer. Leave the cover closed and turn the dryer upside down into the bowl.

Fig. 20-2. Next remove the four recessed screws in the bottom of the dryer.

Fig. 20-3. Remove the nut on the bottom of the fan that holds the impeller in place. Use a screwdriver to turn the slotted shaft the nut is on and a wrench to hold the nut.

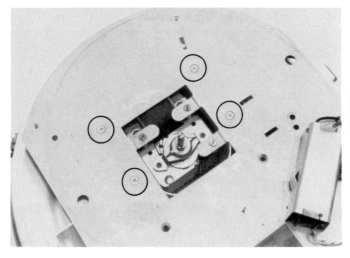

Fig. 20-4. Remove the motor housing and plate by unscrewing the four countersunk Phillips screws in the plate.

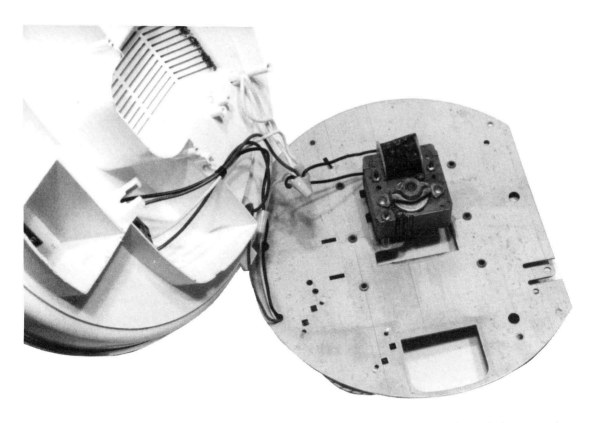

Fig. 20-5. After you remove the plate, inspect the motor and internal wire connection.

Fig. 20-6. Notice the fused strip on the side of the heater cover.

Fig. 20-7. To get to the heating element, bend up the four small tabs that hold the heater cover. Very carefully lift off the cover.

Fig. 20-8. The heating element with the cover removed.

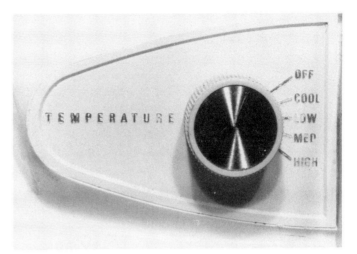

Fig. 20-9. To get to the switch, pry off the control knob from the shaft.

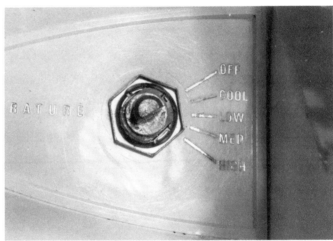

Fig. 20-10. Remove the retaining nut. Label the wires for their proper terminals before you remove the wires.

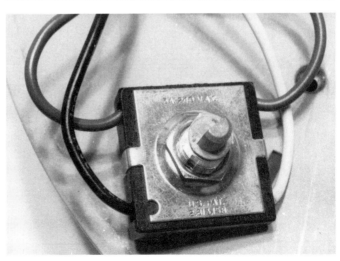

Fig. 20-11. The switch removed from the housing.

HAIR SETTER

Basically, this appliance is just a heating element designed to heat water, which generates steam, which in turn heats rollers in the top of the appliance. These rollers, or curlers, then can be removed and used to set the hair.

Problems from the appliance usually come when minerals are allowed to accumulate inside the unit. To solve this problem, after four to six uses unplug the unit, remove the rollers, and flush the inside with tap water. If the mineral deposit is excessive enough to cause a fuse to blow—an extreme case indeed—fill the unit's measuring cup with warm vinegar, pour in the solution and let it stand for 15 minutes. Next pour out the vinegar and rinse thoroughly with tap water.

Always have the unit unplugged during any washing or cleaning operation. Always use care when using an electrical appliance near water.

A continuity check across the plug terminals will read open on this particular model because the circuit is only complete when there is water in the unit. In this way if the unit runs dry or out of water, it will not heat.

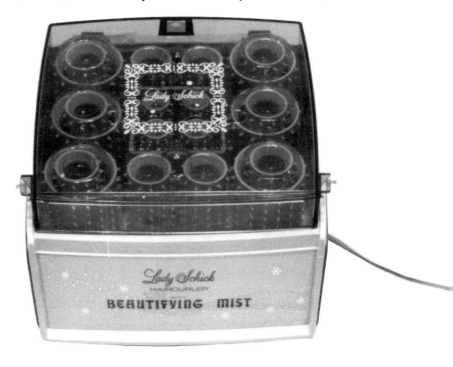

Fig. 21-1. Hair setter.

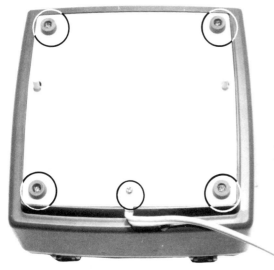

Fig. 21-2. To remove the bottom cover, remove the four Phillips screws inside the feet on the bottom of the appliance and the one Phillips screw by the cord connection. When removing the bottom plate, be careful not to damage the two safety switch buttons sticking through it.

Fig. 21-3. Bottom view of the hair setter with the cover removed.

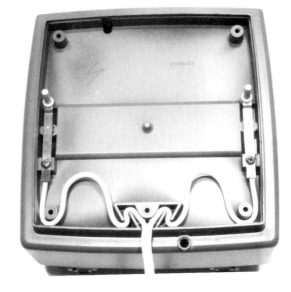

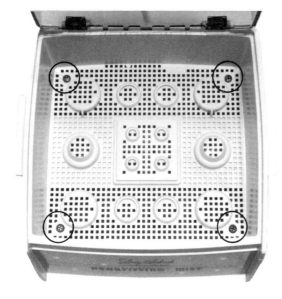

Fig. 21-4. Next remove the four Phillips screws in the top of the housing.

Fig. 21-5. Lift off the perforated cover of the heater, and you will see the elements inside. Notice that they do not touch. They are able to work by conducting through the water in the base.

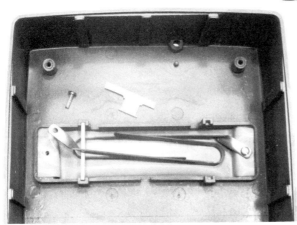

Fig. 21-6. To remove the elements, remove the single screw on the end of each element.

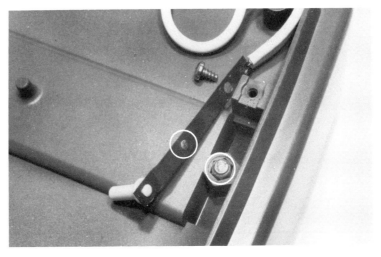

Fig. 21-7. Examine the switch contact by removing the screw holding down the switch arm.

HAIR STYLER

This appliance sees daily use around some households. This model consists of a control handle with a swivel-connected power cord. The on-off switch has two heat positions. The heating element is inside the iron or brush attachment.

Problems with this appliance can usually be found in the power cord or its swivel connection. The frequent use of hair stylers often promotes carelessness. Remember that, even if the switch is off, as long as this appliance is plugged in, it should be considered electrically live. It is also a good idea to move the switch to the off position when changing attachments.

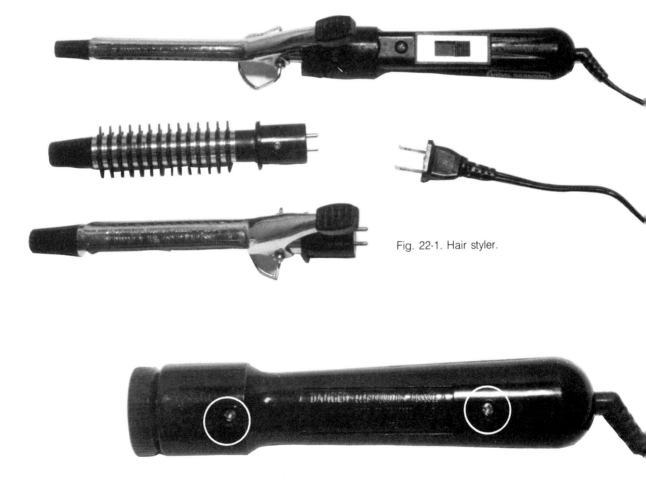

Fig. 22-1. Hair styler.

Fig. 22-2. To get inside the handle, remove the two Phillips screws on the bottom. Next, gently separate the two halves.

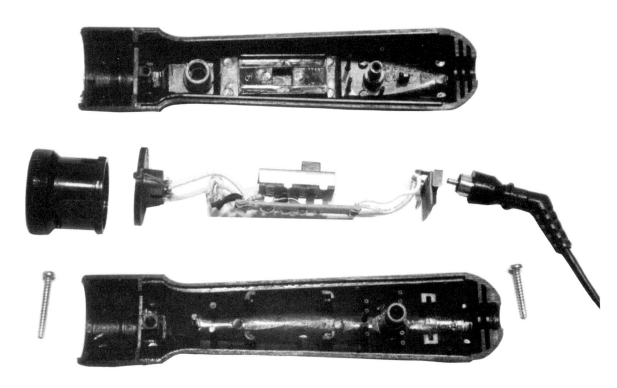

Fig. 22-3. The inside of the hair styler.

Fig. 22-4. Notice the line cord connection. This arrangement allows the cord to swivel while it is being used.

Fig. 22-5. Inspect the switch assembly for broken wires. Also check the indicator lamp.

HEATER, SPACE

Space heaters are useful in providing heat to a limited area. The appliance consists of nothing more than a heating element located in front of a reflector. It is controlled by an on-off switch connected to a line cord. The most common complaint with the appliance is that when it is plugged in and turned on, it often trips a circuit breaker.

This particular heater is rated at 1,000 watts. Using Ohm's Law we divide 1,000 watts by 120 volts and determine that this heater will use about 8.3 amps. This means that when this heater is plugged in to a 20-amp circuit, it will use nearly half the capacity of that circuit. So when this heater is plugged in and turned on, if the breaker trips, it might not be the fault of the heater. Space heaters also are equipped with a safety device that will prevent them from working if they are not in the upright position.

Fig. 23-1. Heater, space.

Fig. 23-2. To get inside, begin by removing the six Phillips screws holding the front grill on. Next, remove the front panel containing the switch assembly.

Fig. 23-3. To remove the switch, gently pry the control knob from the shaft.

Fig. 23-4. Remove the retaining nut from the shaft of the switch.

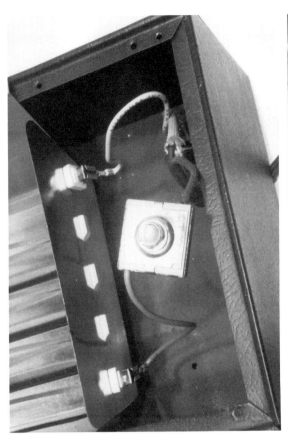

Fig. 23-5. (*left*) The switch removed from the back of the grill.

Fig. 23-6. (*above*) The turnover switch is located inside the frame above the line cord.

Fig. 23-7. (*below*) To remove the level sensor switch, unscrew the Phillips screw from the back of the housing above the line cord's entrance.

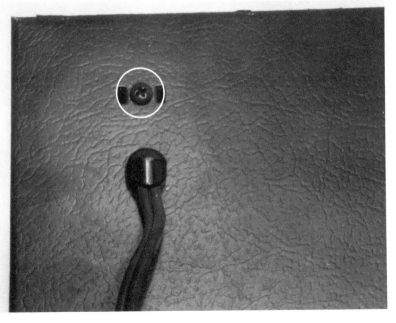

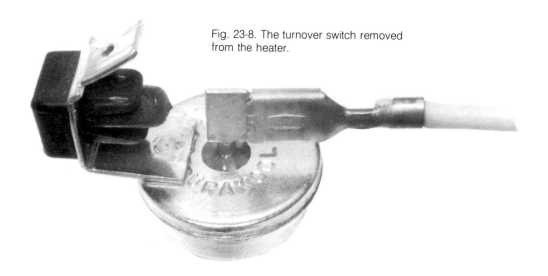

Fig. 23-8. The turnover switch removed from the heater.

Fig. 23-9. Use caution when examining the connections to the heater element. The ceramic insulators that hold the heating element in place inside the reflector are very brittle and easily damaged. After making any repairs and before applying power to this appliance, always make a thorough check for shorts to the frame. Characteristically, these heaters are all metal and, even though the frame is painted, it still can be a good conductor.

HEATER WITH FAN

Even small electric heaters use a large amount of power. One of the most common problems with heaters occurs when they are turned on and they blow a fuse or kick a circuit breaker. Try to plug in heaters where there is little else on the circuit. If you must use an extension cord, make sure it is a heavy-duty type and not the size cord used for lamps. If the cord becomes warm to touch, it is not big enough.

The nature of their use causes heaters to accumulate dust and lint, so an occasional cleaning with a vacuum cleaner will prolong its life. Do not clean or service any appliance while it is plugged in.

Fig. 24-1. Heater with fan.

Fig. 24-2. To get inside this appliance, remove the four recessed screws in the back, then separate the two halves.

Fig. 24-3. Inside view with the back cover removed.

Fig. 24-4. To remove the fan assembly and free the motor and heating element, remove the two Phillips screws in the center of the back.

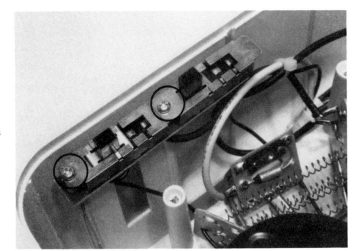

Fig. 24-5. Remove the two small Phillips screws holding the switches in place.

Fig. 24-6. Remove the whole assembly from the housing.

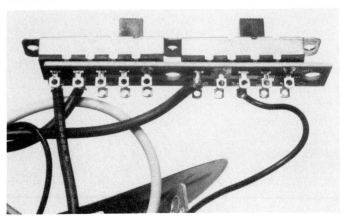

Fig. 24-7. Control switches showing wiring connections.

HEDGE TRIMMER

This appliance can be thought of as a small electric motor that turns a gear. The gear moves one cutting surface back and forth against another, rigid or fixed cutting surface. This operation is controlled by a trigger switch in the handle.

Problems can develop when the hedge trimmer is used to cut too large a twig. A dent in the cutting edge might cause the teeth to bind. If a wire or a rock does put a nick in the blade, you can remove the nick with a fine tooth file. If you accidentally cut the cord, gently put the tool down, go unplug the cord at the outlet, then make your inspection for damage.

Make sure the hedge is dry. Never use an electrical tool in a damp or wet location. Also keep in mind that brushes and motors cause sparks and can ignite fumes such as gasoline.

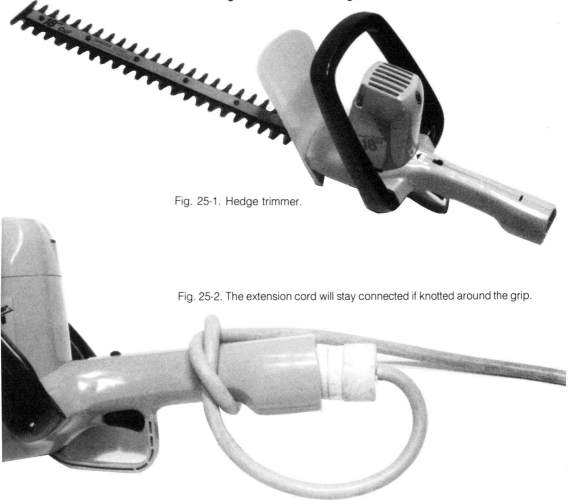

Fig. 25-1. Hedge trimmer.

Fig. 25-2. The extension cord will stay connected if knotted around the grip.

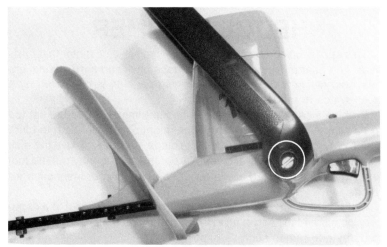

Fig. 25-3. To disassemble this hedge trimmer, first remove the long screw and nut holding the handle in place.

Fig. 25-4. Next remove the three Phillips screws in the top of the motor housing.

Fig. 25-5. Remove the cover and inspect the brushes. If they look okay, do not try to pry them out. If you do, the brush housing will crack and you will need to install new brush assemblies.

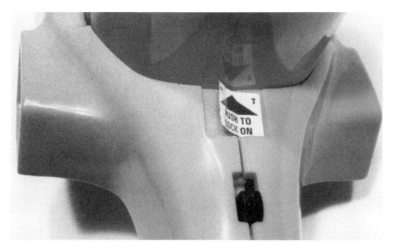

Fig. 25-6. For further disassembly, carefully peel up the switch position decal.

Fig. 25-7. Next, remove the three recessed Phillips screws from the side of the housing.

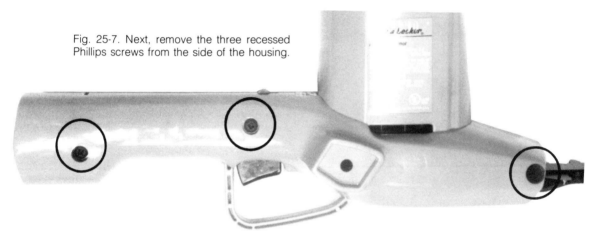

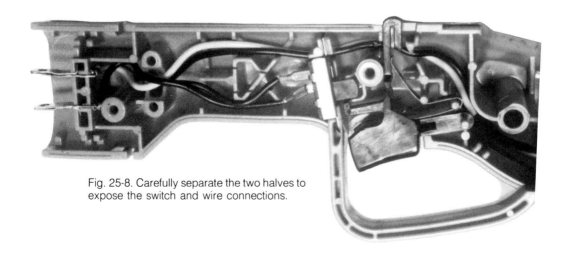

Fig. 25-8. Carefully separate the two halves to expose the switch and wire connections.

Fig. 25-9. To get inside the gear box, remove the four screws in the plate cover.

Fig. 25-10. (*below center*) The drive gear with the plate removed.

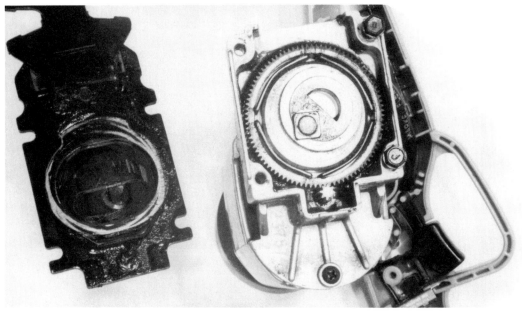

Fig. 25-11. Remove the other Phillips screw and remove the armature (illustrated showing normal wear on the commutator).

ICE CREAM MAKER

This appliance consists of a motor connected to a line cord controlled by an on-off switch. The top portion of the appliance contains an inner and outer drum. When the area between the two drums is packed with a mixture of ice and table salt and the switch is turned on, the motor will rotate the inner drum, freezing its contents. This appliance's use can be considered seasonal and should provide years of service.

The motor and the switch is located in the base and offers easy access. Problems could occur in the line cord or the switch, but most problems will probably be related to the motor or the gears. If you exercise care to keep the motor from being overloaded, however, this appliance can be a worthwhile addition to any household.

Fig. 26-1. Ice cream maker.

Fig. 26-2. The motor and switch are housed in the base.

Fig. 26-3. Feet plugs conceal the recessed Phillips screws that hold the bottom cover in place. Pry out the four rubber feet and remove the four deeply recessed screws.

Fig. 26-4. Remove cover and notice the strain relief knot on the housing bracket. Make sure it is in place when you reassemble the appliance. Remove the three Phillips screws that hold the motor and gear assembly in place.

Fig. 26-5. Lift out the motor and gear assembly.

Fig. 26-6. The switch is held in place with a tab on each end. Compress the ends of the switch, and the switch will pop through the housing.

IRON, STEAM

There are two types of irons: a steam iron and a dry iron. Electrically there is little or no difference between the two. The electrical part is very simple, consisting of a heating element controlled by a thermostat. The difference between the two types is that the steam iron must contain some type of small reservoir that can be filled with water. It also must have some type of control valve that allows a small amount of water to travel to the bottom of the iron to the sole plate. At this point, heat from the heating element converts the water into steam, which then escapes through the ports in the bottom of the sole plate.

Problems can occur when the iron accidentally slides from the ironing board, causing an undue strain on the power cord or breaking the handle. The metal tab of a zipper could scratch the sole plate deep enough to cause snagging. Rubbing with steel wool will help here. Avoid disconnecting the iron from the wall outlet by jerking on the cord.

Other problems could occur from a defective switch or thermostat. Seldom the heating elements themselves cause any problem. The most common problem with irons is caused by mineral buildup, which begins to restrict the flow of steam through the bottom of the iron. Continued buildup will eventually plug some of the ports.

Fig. 27-1. Iron, steam.

Use distilled water in steam irons. If the ports do become plugged, use a straightened paper clip to open the holes, then flush the tank with a solution of equal parts of vinegar and water. Pour the solution into the iron and then set the iron on its lowest steam setting. Then while the iron is heating, place a clean wire rack, something with feet on it like a cake rack, over an old towel. Next place the iron flat on the rack and steam a full tank of the vinegar water solution through the iron. Finish the cleaning by flushing the tank with clean water until there is no more vinegar smell.

Irons are sometimes tricky to get apart, and they are even harder to get back together. Disassemble the iron in a sequence, laying parts out in the order that you remove them. Work slowly and don't force anything.

Fig. 27-2. To examine the cord connection, begin by removing the recessed screw in the cord plate. This one required an allen wrench, and a small pin in the middle of the screw head had to be broken off in order to accept the wrench.

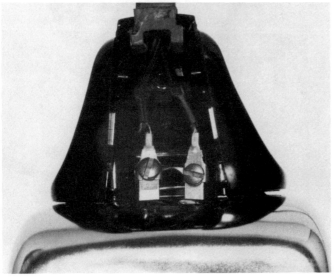

Fig. 27-3. Remove the cover and inspect the wire connections.

Fig. 27-4. To get inside the base, pry off the saddle plate in the handle.

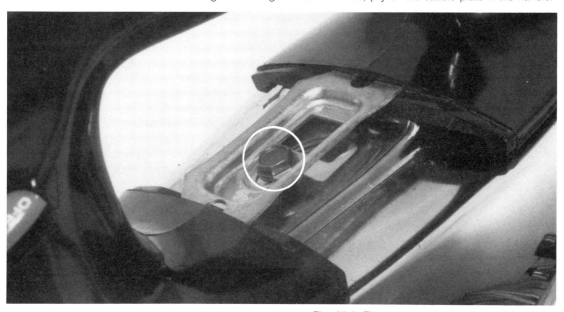

Fig. 27-5. Then remove the handle retaining bolt.

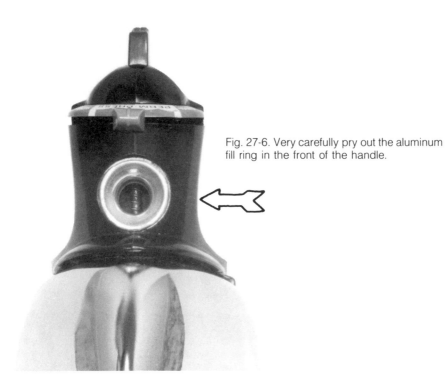

Fig. 27-6. Very carefully pry out the aluminum fill ring in the front of the handle.

Fig. 27-7. Lift off the handle
and top of the iron, exposing the tank.
Remove the screw on the front point of the
base and lift off the retaining bracket and tank.

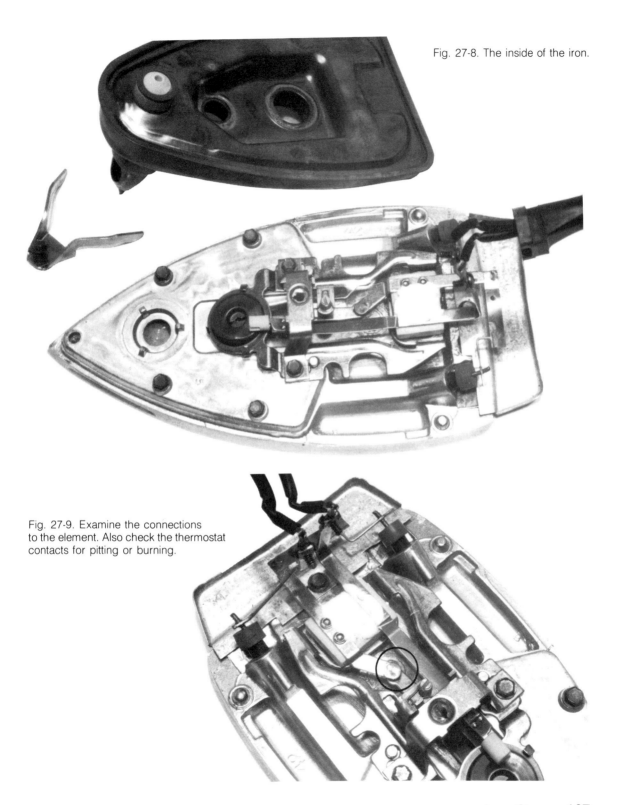

Fig. 27-8. The inside of the iron.

Fig. 27-9. Examine the connections to the element. Also check the thermostat contacts for pitting or burning.

JUICER

This handy appliance is very simple and consists of nothing more than a motor connected to a spring-loaded shaft, which fits inside a reamer. When one-half of a citrus fruit is pressed down on the top of this reamer, it activates a switch, which automatically starts the motor. When the fruit is lifted from the reamer, the action stops. The motor does not drive the shaft directly, but is connected to it through a series of reduction gears to increase the power. They also reduce the speed of the shaft.

Most problems occur from a buildup of pulp around the shaft area. This buildup decreases the performance of the juicer and eventually could cause it to fail altogether. Usually, all that is necessary is a thorough cleaning. To clean the base, wipe with a damp cloth; never immerse the base in water. Wash the rest of the juicer parts in hot, soapy water. It is better to wash them by hand and not use the dishwasher.

Juicers tend to perform better when the fruit is at room temperature. It also helps if you roll the fruit between the palm of your hand and a countertop before cutting. This action helps loosen the fibers inside.

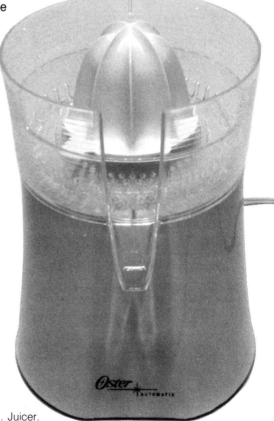

Fig. 28-1. Juicer.

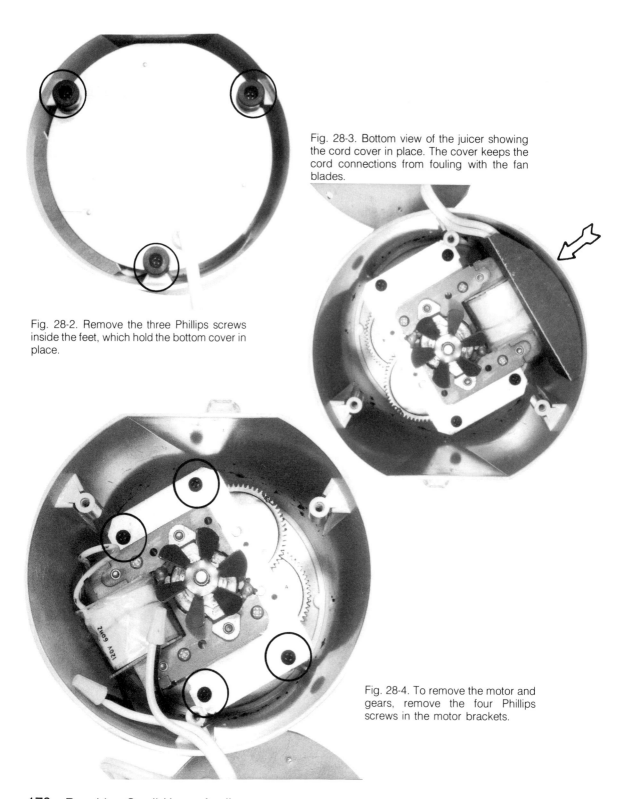

Fig. 28-2. Remove the three Phillips screws inside the feet, which hold the bottom cover in place.

Fig. 28-3. Bottom view of the juicer showing the cord cover in place. The cover keeps the cord connections from fouling with the fan blades.

Fig. 28-4. To remove the motor and gears, remove the four Phillips screws in the motor brackets.

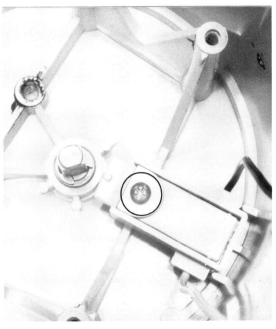

Fig. 28-5. Next remove the snap ring holding the gear to the coupling.

Fig. 28-6. After the gear is removed, remove the switch. It is held in place by a single Phillips screw.

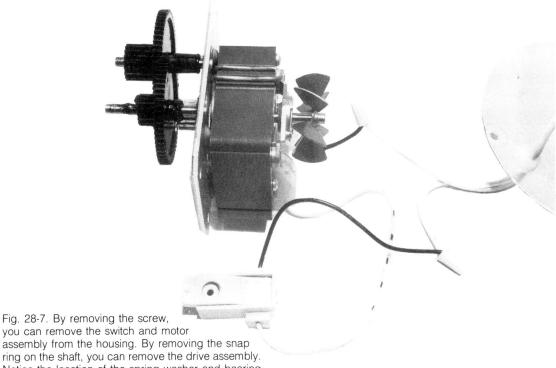

Fig. 28-7. By removing the screw, you can remove the switch and motor assembly from the housing. By removing the snap ring on the shaft, you can remove the drive assembly. Notice the location of the spring washer and bearing.

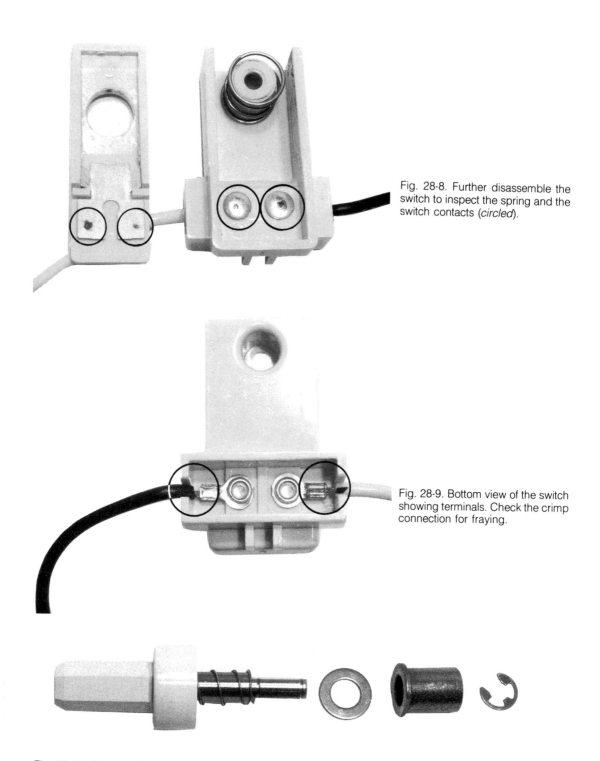

Fig. 28-8. Further disassemble the switch to inspect the spring and the switch contacts (*circled*).

Fig. 28-9. Bottom view of the switch showing terminals. Check the crimp connection for fraying.

Fig. 28-10. The coupling removed from the housing.

LAWN EDGER

This powerful tool is a great labor-saving device for trimming the lawn around walks and driveways. It basically consists of a motor mounted sideways, driving reduction gears that are connected to a small blade. This model has a tilt position, which allows the motor and cutting-head assembly to swivel. This swiveling enables the edger to perform small trenching operations. Power to the motor is supplied by wires fed through the tube and connected to a trigger switch in the handle.

The switch or motor seldom causes any problems, but after many seasons of use the motor brushes might need some attention. Most problems are related to the operation of the blade when it strikes the edge of the pavement or becomes entangled in a foreign object. This could cause it to bend or even break. Let the tool cut at its own pace. If forced at a higher pace, an excessive load is placed on the motor and the life of the gears will be greatly shortened.

When you are operating the edger, a stone at just the right angle can become a high-speed missile. Therefore, you should wear safety goggles and keep bystanders kept out of the work area. If soil conditions cause the blade chamber to be clogged, first unplug the tool, then open the blade guard. With a stick or an old screwdriver, remove the clogged material. Sprinkler heads are often located along sidewalks and driveways. You might want to trim around these by hand because the blade can easily destroy these fittings. It is tempting to abuse this tool because of the nature of its jobs, but with careful use, the lawn edger should provide years of trouble-free service.

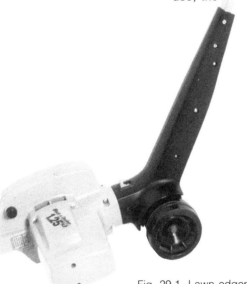

Fig. 29-1. Lawn edger.

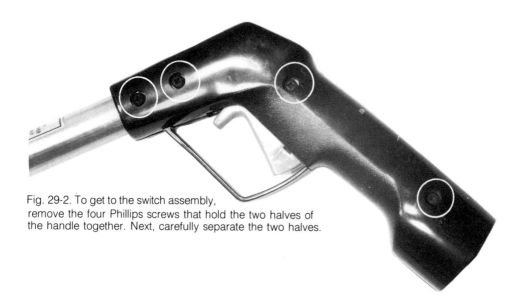

Fig. 29-2. To get to the switch assembly,
remove the four Phillips screws that hold the two halves of
the handle together. Next, carefully separate the two halves.

Fig. 29-3. Inside view of the handle, showing the trigger switch and
wiring. Before removing the switch, notice the routing of the wires. They
must be in the same position for reassembly or
the two halves of the handle will not fit together.

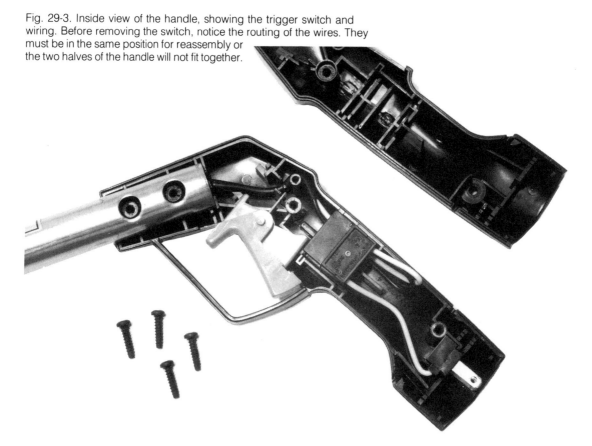

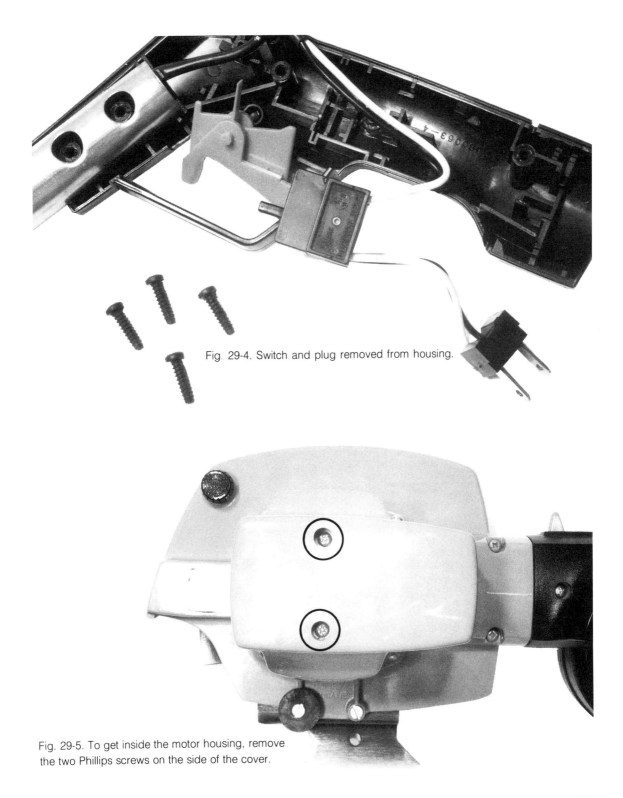

Fig. 29-4. Switch and plug removed from housing.

Fig. 29-5. To get inside the motor housing, remove
the two Phillips screws on the side of the cover.

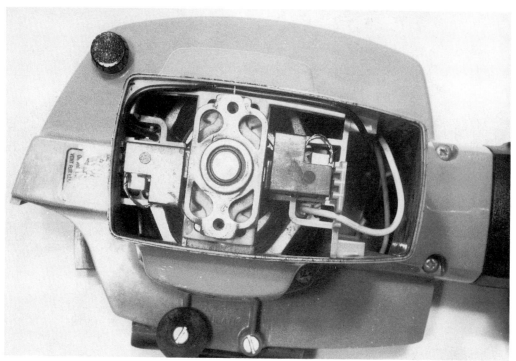

Fig. 29-6. Top view of the motor, showing brush assemblies.

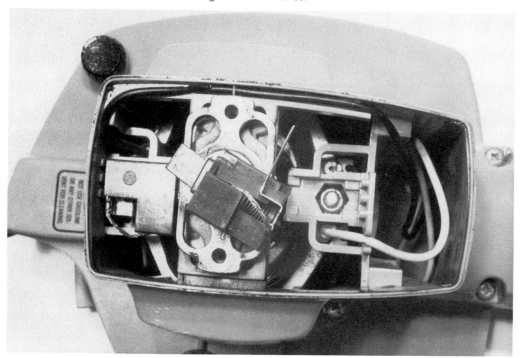

Fig. 29-7. Remove the cover and gently lift out the brushes for inspection.

Fig. 29-8. Next lift off the top bearing and spacers from the motor.

Fig. 29-9. Remove the six Phillips screws from around the motor housing. (Two are shown.)

Fig. 29-10. Remove the housing. It is held in place by four nuts located just behind the blade. Next remove the blades.

Fig. 29-11. Remove the four Phillips screws holding the gear cover in place.

Fig. 29-12. Remove the cover to expose the gears for inspection and removal.

Fig. 29-13. Gear removed for inspection. Look for worn or missing teeth.

Fig. 29-14. Bottom view of gear housing containing the motor bearing.

Fig. 29-15. Remove the fan shroud, then the armature and fan.

Lawn Edger 179

LAWN MOWER

Electric lawn mowers are becoming more popular in areas where noise pollution is a problem. They also eliminate the hazards of storing a gasoline can, and they rarely fail to start the first time. The big disadvantages of electric mowers are the extension cord and the hazards of shock if the mower is operated in the rain or on wet locations.

A control switch in the handle controls the motor, which is mounted in a vertical position and is directly connected to the cutting blade. The handle on this model flips over so that the mower can be operated without changing directions in a back-and-forth pattern, rather than the conventional square pattern. This pattern keeps the power cord on the same side all the time and reduces the hazard of running over the cord with the mower.

The most common problems are related to the blade area. Grass can build up enough to clog the discharge opening, and occasionally the blade should be sharpened. After many seasons of use, problems with the motor might be caused by worn brushes.

Before storing the motor for the winter, it is a good practice to lubricate the motor bearing. Simply remove the motor cover and drop five drops of oil in the felt reservoir at the top of the motor, then replace the cover.

Fig. 30-1. Lawn mower.

Fig. 30-2. To get to the switch assembly, remove the six Phillips screws in the side of the housing that hold the two halves of the control switch together.

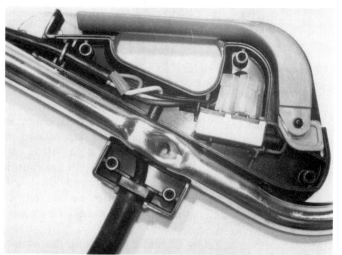

Fig. 30-3. Gently separate the two halves. Inspect the switch and its associated wiring.

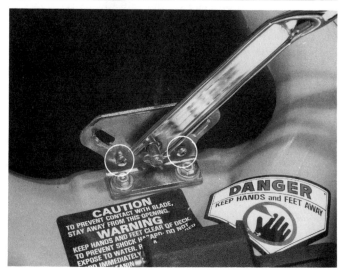

Fig. 30-4. To get to the motor area, removing the two screws in each side of the motor housing that hold the motor cover in place.

Fig. 30-5. Top view of the motor. Remove the two Phillips screws holding the brush assemblies in place.

Fig. 30-6. Examine the brush assemblies.

Fig. 30-7. For further disassembly, you must remove the blade. Simply hold the blade and remove the nut with a wrench.

Fig. 30-8. Bottom view of the motor with the blade removed. Unscrew the four motor mount bolts.

Fig. 30-9. Next, remove the two bolts alongside the motor shaft holding the housing in place.

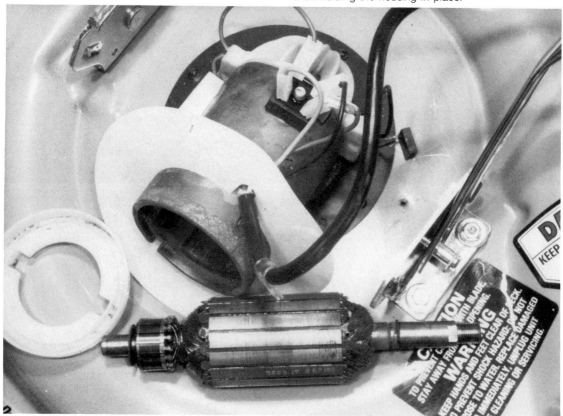

Fig. 30-10. Now lift the armature free of the motor housing and inspect it.

MIXER

There are two types of mixers found in today's kitchens: The stand model, and the portable hand-held mixer. They both operate on the same principle. This appliance consists of a line cord connected to a motor that is controlled by a variable-speed selector switch. The end of the motor shaft is really a worm gear, which drives two counterrotating gears that turn the beaters.

Most problems develop from bent or damaged beaters, with occasional problems from faulty line cords. The hand-held mixer is usually not as powerful as the stand model and therefore should be limited to the lighter liquid mixes. The gears seem to stand up well, but with extensive use the control switch might cause problems and the brushes might need attention. Use care not to force the beaters into their sockets. If installed incorrectly the beaters will strike each other, damaging the beaters and possibly the gears. This problem is usually solved by keeping the sockets cleaned. Here a toothpick works very well.

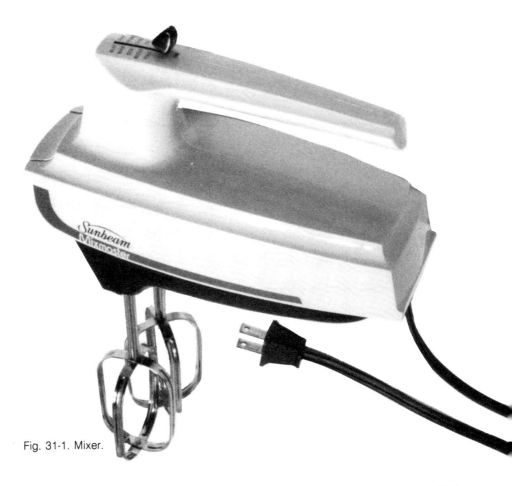

Fig. 31-1. Mixer.

Fig. 31-2. Mixer control switch.

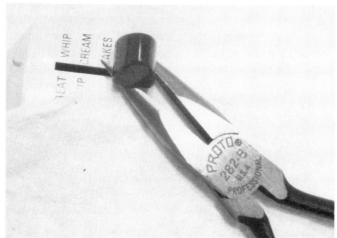

Fig. 31-3. To get inside the mixer, begin by prying the knob from the selector switch. It is a good idea to use a paper towel or something soft to keep from scratching the appliance.

Fig. 31-4. Next remove the four Phillips screws in the bottom and separate the two halves.

Fig. 31-5. Inside view of the mixer.

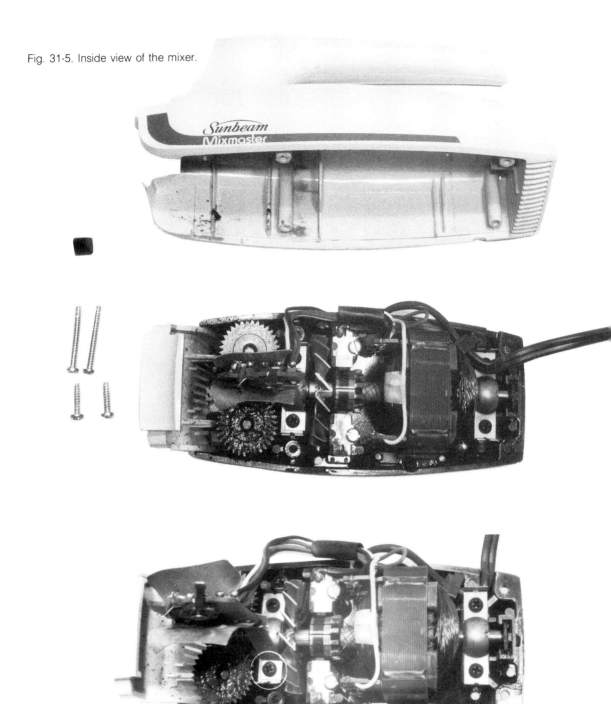

Fig. 31-6. Take out the selector switch by removing the one Phillips screw in the switch bracket that holds the switch to the base.

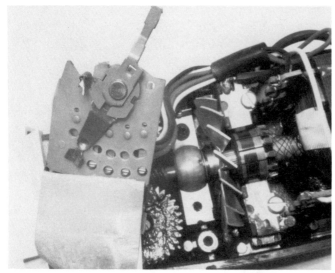

Fig. 31-7. Peel back the switch cover to inspect the switch contacts.

Fig. 31-8. Loosen the two brush holder retaining screws and examine the brushes.

Fig. 31-9. To remove the motor, next remove the single Phillips screws on the front bearing strap, the two Phillips screws on the back bearing strap, and the two retaining screws on the side of the motor.

Fig. 31-10. Lift out the motor and switch assembly from the housing.

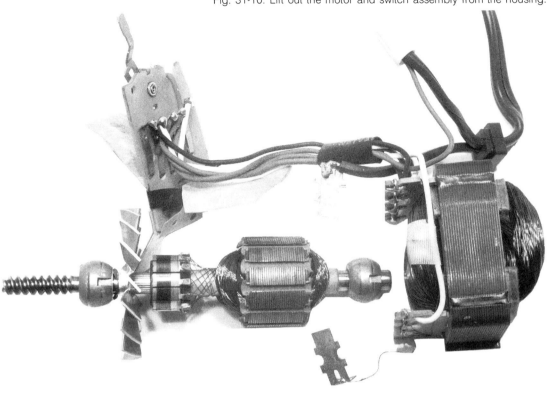

Fig. 31-11. A spring is used to keep tension on the mixer blade ejector.

SPRING

OVEN, TOASTER-BROILER

This countertop appliance is actually a scaled-down version of the ovens found in electric ranges. It is a simple appliance and consists of a heating element, which is controlled by a thermostat connected to a power cord. On this model, the temperature control knob is connected directly to the thermostat.

The heating element seldom becomes defective. The most likely trouble spot tends to be the thermostat. Usually the contacts become pitted, which prevents the elements from heating properly. Because these appliances are all metal and they draw a large amount of current, be careful to make a thorough check for any shorts to ground after you make any repair.

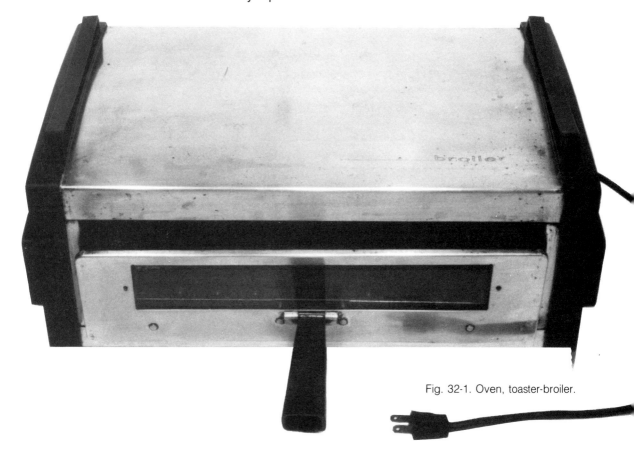

Fig. 32-1. Oven, toaster-broiler.

Fig. 32-2. To get inside the toaster oven, first gently pry the control knob from the shaft.

Fig. 32-3. Next remove the two outside screws inside the oven. Separate the two halves. The center screw of the three screws inside the oven holds the thermostat control. Remove this screw.

Fig. 32-4. Inside view showing the thermostat control and the connections to the heating element. Remove the control for inpsection. Carefully remove the screws to the terminals of the element.

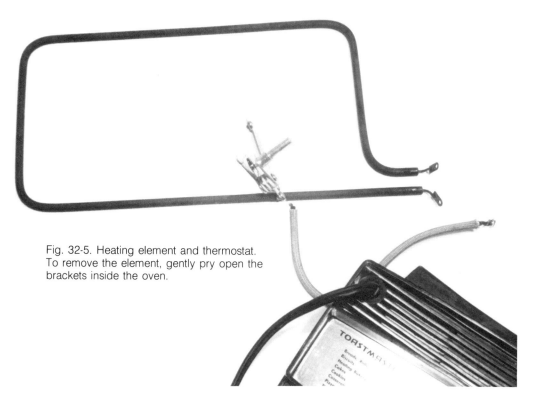

Fig. 32-5. Heating element and thermostat. To remove the element, gently pry open the brackets inside the oven.

POPCORN POPPER

The popularity of hot-air popcorn poppers is growing, partly because they cook without oil, so extra calories are not added. Generally, however, their popularity stems from the fact that the kernels are popped more quickly and efficiently. This appliance normally receives only occasional use, and consequently tends to last for years without problems.

It basically consists of a line cord connected to a blower motor and heating element. The blower motor assembly forces air around the heating element and up into the popping chamber. The air then flows up into the cover and is channeled out through a shoot. When the kernels

Fig. 33-1. Popcorn popper.

are placed in the popping chamber, the heated air bounces the kernels around some but is not able to lift them very high. When the kernel pops, the increased size allows it to be quickly blown out the shoot.

On this model, the thermostat is designed to shut off the appliance to prevent overheating if the popping chamber is overfilled, or if the appliance is used repeatedly without a cooling-off period. Should this happen, simply unplug the popper from the wall outlet. Remove the cover and empty the popping chamber of any kernels and allow the appliance to cool for about 15 minutes before using again.

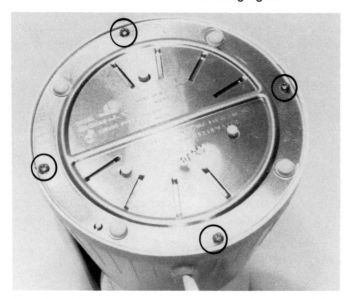

Fig. 33-2. To get inside the popcorn popper, remove the four Phillips screws on the bottom that hold the bottom cover in place. You now will have access to the cord connection, as well as to the connections to the heater and motor.

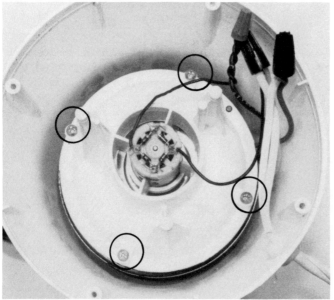

Fig. 33-3. For further disassembly, remove the four Phillips screws on the fan housing holding the motor assembly in place.

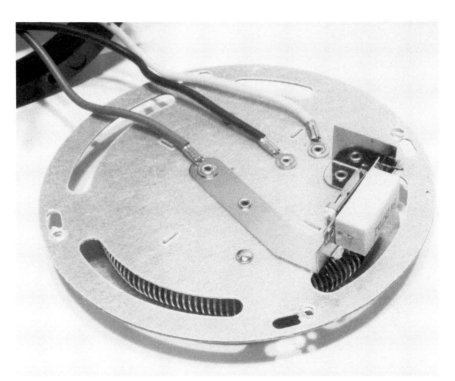

Fig. 33-4. Now lift up the remaining components for inspection. The heating element with wire connections is shown.

Fig. 33-5. The impeller is permanently bradded to the shaft and cannot be removed.

RAZOR

Electric razors can be considered in two classes: those using a rotary motor, and those using a vibrator motor. Line cords seldom pose a problem, and the motors are very reliable. Most of the problems occur around the cutting heads. Rotor motors have two kinds of cutting heads: one moving the cutters back and forth in opposition to each other, and the other spinning cutting wheels inside round heads called *combs*. The vibrator motor operates 60 times a second, regulated by the 60 hertz established in the household circuit.

Although outwardly rugged, the internal parts of a razor are quite delicate. Most manufacturers prefer the appliance to be returned to them for repairs. Almost all of the repairs can be avoided by a regular cleaning schedule.

Fig. 34-1. Razor.

Fig. 34-2. Bottom view of the razor showing the voltage selector switch.

Fig. 34-3. To disassemble this appliance, gently lift off the blade assembly, which is held in place by a spring-loaded clip.

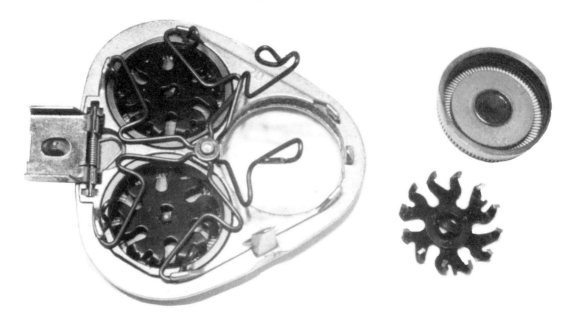

Fig. 34-4. To remove the cutting blades and the comb, compress the retaining clip.

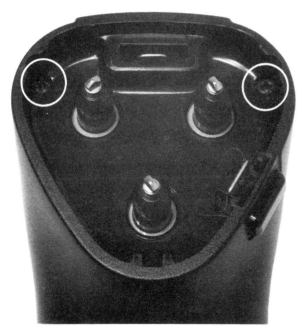

Fig. 34-5. To get inside the housing, remove the two Phillips screws in the top.

Fig. 34-6. To complete the separation of the housing, remove the Phillips screw in the handle at the lower part of the housing. Next carefully separate the two halves.

Fig. 34-7. The trimmer is held in place by an S-shaped retaining spring and fits in notches in the housing.

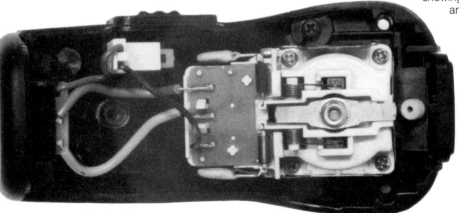

Fig. 34-8. (*center*) Inside view of the razor showing a motor and switch.

Fig. 34-9. To remove the motor and gear assembly, remove the two Phillips screws on the side.

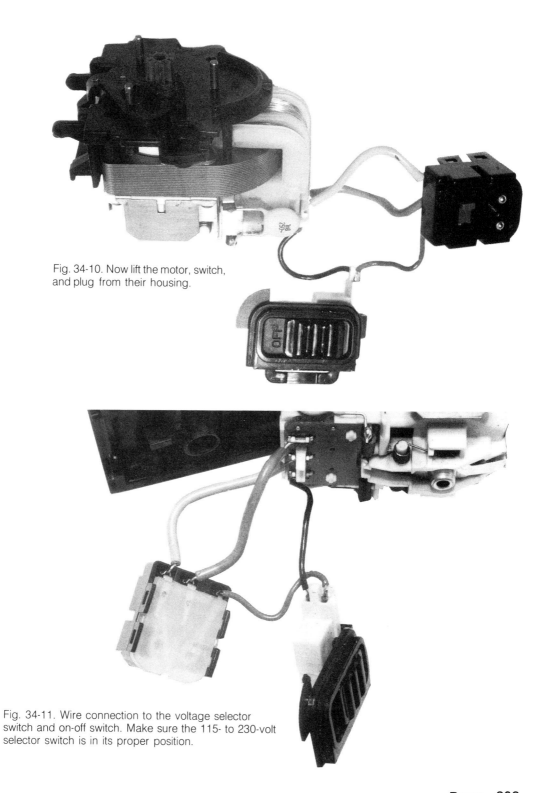

Fig. 34-10. Now lift the motor, switch, and plug from their housing.

Fig. 34-11. Wire connection to the voltage selector switch and on-off switch. Make sure the 115- to 230-volt selector switch is in its proper position.

Fig. 34-12. Razor disassembled.

SABER SAW

This compact, lightweight tool can be fitted with a variety of blades to accommodate different cutting needs. The operation consists of a line cord supplying power to a motor controlled by a switch. The motor shaft turns a gear that moves another shaft up and down. The shaft is connected to the cutting blade.

An abused line cord can cause problems, and occasionally the switches become defective. Generally, however, the most frequent problems are related to an accumulation and buildup of dust inside the motor housing and around the reciprocation shaft assembly.

Excessive sparking in the motor could indicate bad brushes. If the motor hums but the blade doesn't move, take a look at the gears to see if they are jammed. With any lightweight cutting tool, such as a drill or saw, a dull blade will increase the temptation to apply excessive force to get the tool to cut. This excessive force, if continued, can quickly burn out a motor and damage the gears. This small power tool is normally used only occasionally. If you keep it reasonably clean and use sharp blades, it should provide many years of trouble-free service.

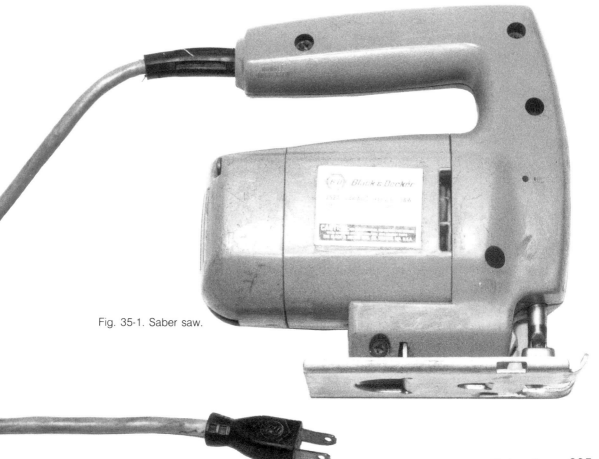

Fig. 35-1. Saber saw.

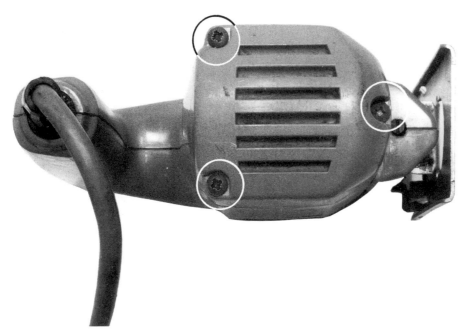

Fig. 35-2. To get to the brushes, remove the three Phillips screws on the end of the housing. These three screws also hold on the motor assembly.

Fig. 35-3. With the back cover removed, you can now gently pry out the brush holder.

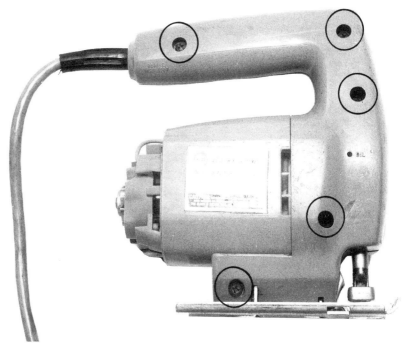

Fig. 35-4. To get to the switch area, remove the five Phillips screws recessed in the side of the handle assembly. Next, carefully separate the two halves.

Fig. 35-5. Inside view showing the reciprocating shaft and switch wiring.

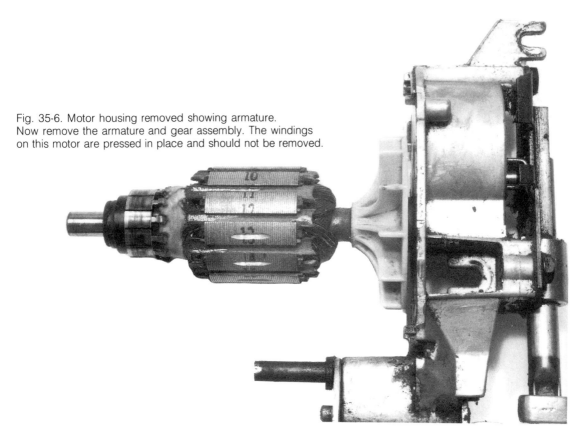

Fig. 35-6. Motor housing removed showing armature. Now remove the armature and gear assembly. The windings on this motor are pressed in place and should not be removed.

Fig. 35-7. To get to the gears, remove the three retaining screws and carefully remove the shaft assembly.

208   Repairing Small Home Appliances

Fig. 35-8. Reciprocating shaft and gear.

Fig. 35-9. Remove the gear for inspection.

SLOW COOKER

This appliance consists of a heating element whose temperature is regulated by a control knob connected directly to a thermostat. The heating element is not sealed, so you should never immerse the appliance in water. This model has a detachable line cord.

The start-up procedure, as with any appliance with a detachable line cord, is to have the control switch in the off position. Next connect the cord to the appliance and then to the wall outlet. Then turn on the appliance to start the operation.

Most problems with this appliance result from a defective thermostat, but occasionally the heating elements do burn out. Take care when making repairs that all insulating devices are intact. Be sure to perform a thorough continuity check for shorts to ground after you make the repair and before you connect the appliance to a power source.

Fig. 36-1. Slow cooker.

Fig. 36-2. Base of the slow cooker, containing the heating element and control switch.

Fig. 36-3. To look at the inside of this appliance, begin by gently prying off the control knob from the switch shaft.

Fig. 36-4. Next, remove the retaining nut on the bottom of the appliance.

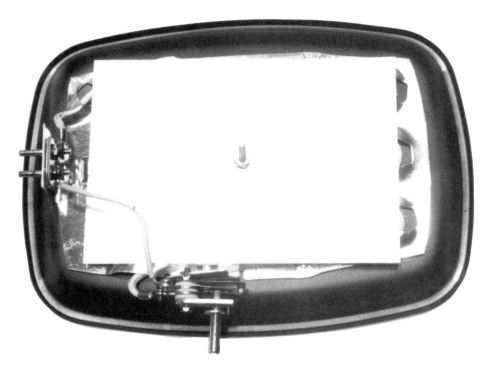

Fig. 36-5. Inside view showing the thermostat and plate covering the heating element.

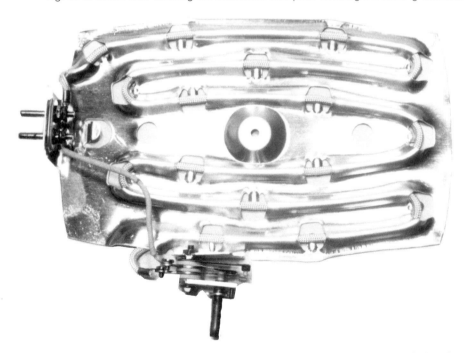

Fig. 36-6. After removing the plate over the heating element, lift out the entire heating element and thermostat control for inspection.

Fig. 36-7. Inspect the contacts on the thermostat control for burning or pitting.

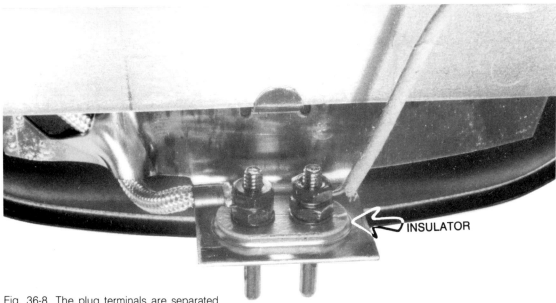

INSULATOR

Fig. 36-8. The plug terminals are separated from the housing by an insulator. Check the plug receptacle for damage to the insulation behind the nut.

TELEPHONE

Telephones are one of the most used appliances around the home. A quality telephone is almost an indestructible piece of equipment. Problems that do occur, primarily tend to be related to faulty cords, either between the base and the hand piece or between the base and the wall jack. After years of extensive use in dusty or otherwise adverse environments, the push-button switches can be clogged and fail to respond. Often, such problems can be solved with a spray contact cleaner without even opening up the base.

If the telephone is "dead," first try another wall jack. Then substitute a known good cord. This cord usually will locate the problem. If you must open the base, be prepared to work with, or around, very small gauge wiring.

Fig. 37-1. Telephone.

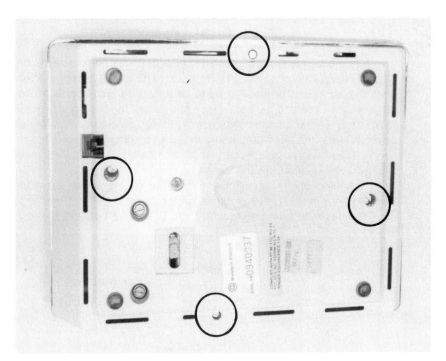

Fig. 37-2. To open the base, begin by removing the two recessed screws on the sides and the two outside screws on the top and bottom.

Fig. 37-3. Next carefully pry off the cover to expose the switch assembly, its associated wiring, and the bell.

Fig. 37-4. To remove the push-button switch assembly, unscrew the four screws on the switch bracket. Next, lift the switch assembly and its bracket from the housing.

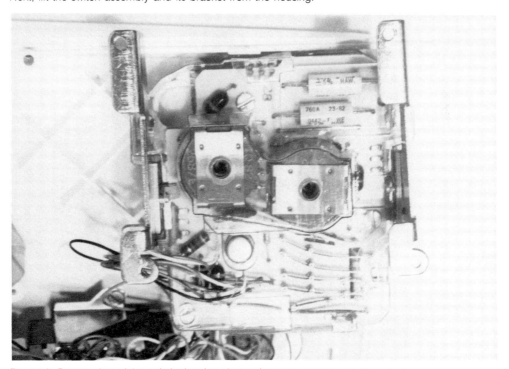

Fig. 37-5. Bottom view of the switch showing electronic components inside the plastic cover.

Fig. 37-6. The plastic dust cover protects the switch from dust particles and helps give it a longer life. Loosen the two screws on the side of the switch assembly and remove the plastic dust guard and the bracket.

Fig. 37-7. Notice the locator pins on the side of the switch assembly. They will line up with the holes in the switch bracket.

Fig. 37-8. For further disassembly of the switch, remove the four outside screws on the bottom of the switch assembly.

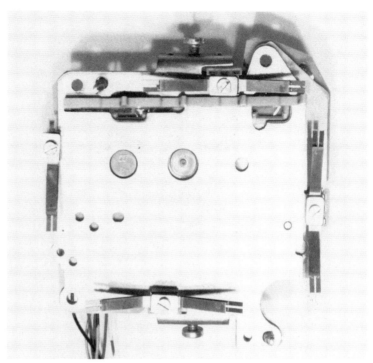

Fig. 37-9. Inside view of the switch showing contacts.

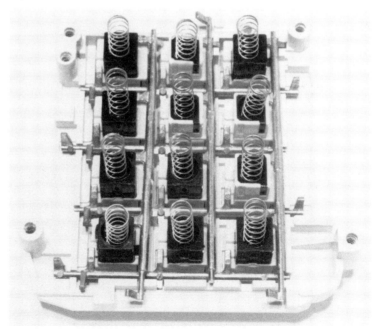

Fig. 37-10. Next very carefully and slowly lift off the bottom half of the switch. The back side of the push buttons and their springs are now open for inspection.

Fig. 37-11. Keep in mind that the remaining parts are held in place by gravity alone. Gently lift off the guide plate to expose the rods that activate the different sets of contactors. It is critical that they fit in their selective notches between the push buttons.

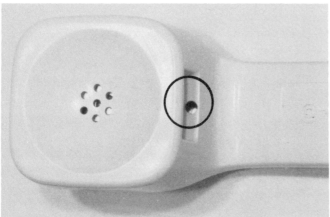

Fig. 37-12. To get inside the handset, remove the deeply recessed screw next to the receiver. Then gently pry off the cover.

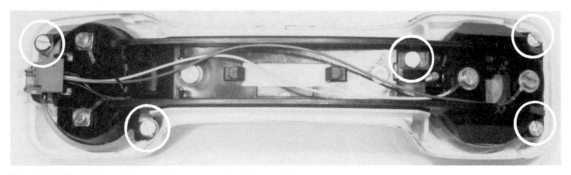

Fig. 37-13. For further disassembly, remove the five retaining screws.

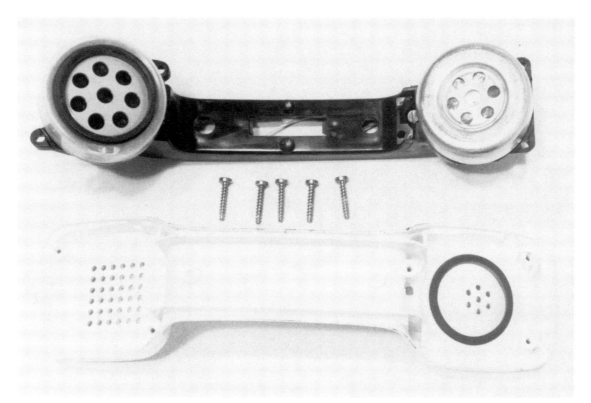

Fig. 37-14. Handset with its cover removed.

Fig. 37-15. The mouthpiece or transmitter is held in place by a flexible ring. Remove the mouthpiece cover.

Fig. 37-16. To get to the transmitter contacts, simply pry off the mouthpiece.

Fig. 37-17. To remove the receiver, remove the two wire terminal screws and lift off the earpiece.

Fig. 37-18. Back view of transmitting unit.

TIRE INFLATER

With the increasing number of self-service gas stations, these handy devices are becoming more popular with the general public. Although primarily used in emergencies, they perform well in keeping tires properly inflated to minimize tire wear and increase fuel efficiency.

The most common problem occurs when the compressor is run continually. The motors tend to overheat and burn out. In most cases, when the motor burns out, it is more practical to replace the entire unit than to try to repair the motor.

These small compressors tend not to receive a lot of use, so they should provide years of insurance against getting stuck with a low tire. Probably the biggest influence in the life of the compressor is to allow it to cool between operations.

Fig. 38-1. Tire inflater.

Fig. 38-2. To replace the lamp on this model, pop off the outer cover.

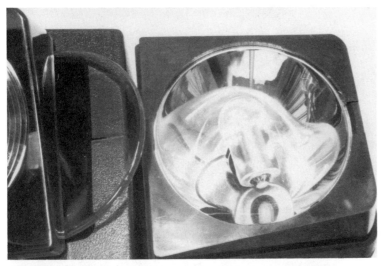

Fig. 38-3. Use a small screwdriver or a pocketknife to pry out the lens cover. Replace the bulb.

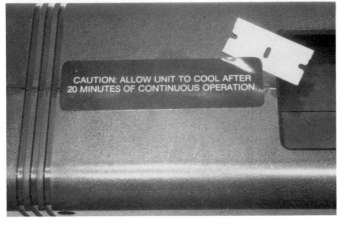

Fig. 38-4. To separate the two halves of the housing, peel the label from the bottom of the unit.

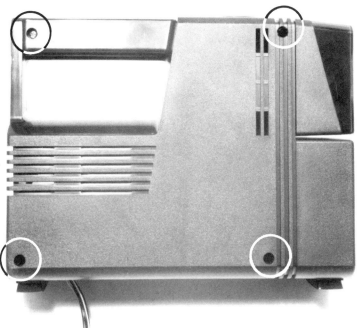

Fig. 38-5. Remove the four Phillips screws holding the side panels together.

Fig. 38-6. Inside view of the tire inflater.

Fig. 38-7. Next remove the side panel, exposing the compressor assembly. Lift off the compressor with its pressure gauge from the housing.

Fig. 38-8. This simple compressor, or air pump, operates when the motor turns a gear connected to a cam that moves a piston back and forth inside a cylinder.

Fig. 38-9. To get to the piston, remove the three screws on the top of the compressor that connect the top of the cylinder, and lift off the top.

Fig. 38-10. The compressor disassembled. If the cylinder walls and piston become dirty, wipe them clean and relubricate them with some petroleum jelly.

Fig. 38-11. Peel back the flexible cover surrounding the gauge. To remove the gauge, slide back the wire wrapping next to the gauge fitting, which is actually a hose clamp.

Fig. 38-12. Barbed tube fitting on the back of the pressure gauge.

Fig. 38-13. Back view of the lamp showing the wire connections. Occasionally, the electrical connections to the back of the lamp become corroded and provide poor connections. Keep them clean and shiny.

Fig. 38-14. Wire connections to switch terminals. To remove the switches, first remove the lugs, then compress the ends of the switch, allowing it to pop free from the housing.

Fig. 38-15. Notice that the terminals on the switch are not separated evenly. This uneven spacing helps you determine how to replace the switch properly.

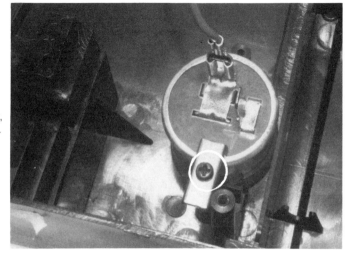

Fig. 38-16. To remove the emergency flasher, loosen the Phillips screw holding the clamp.

Fig. 38-17. The flasher unit is marked to ensure proper replacement.

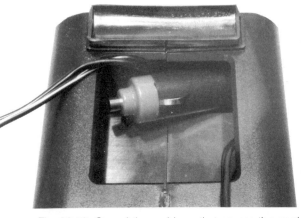

Fig. 38-18. One of the problems that causes the cord to fail is created by the cord's cramped storage compartment. When storing the cord, place the plug in the compartment first.

Fig. 38-19. Next fold the cord in equal sections behind the plug.

TOASTER

One of the most popular and frequently used household appliances is the toaster. The most common model is one in which the bread is placed in a slot containing a rack that is located between two heating elements. On the model illustrated, the bread lowers automatically. On others, however, a lever is depressed starting a timing device and turning on the heating elements for a predetermined length of time. At the end of this period, a latch is released, turning off the heating elements.

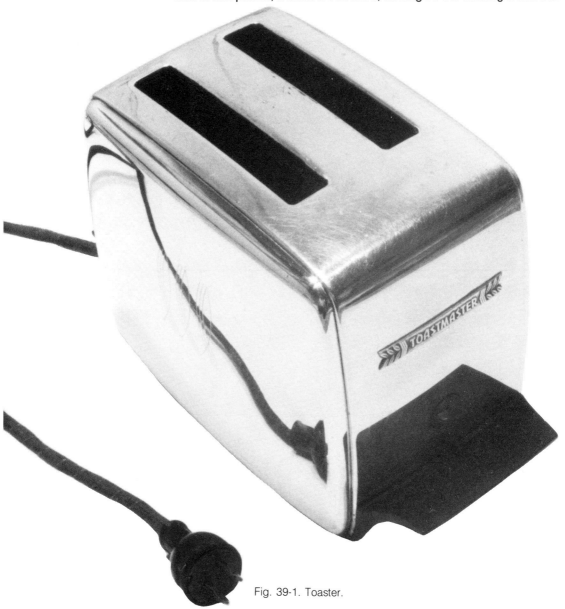

Fig. 39-1. Toaster.

The rack then raises the bread in the slot high enough to be retrieved by the user. The temperature of the heating elements is controlled by an adjustable thermostat set by a dark-light selector knob.

Most toasters tend to operate for many years before problems occur, then a buildup of bread crumbs can cause the mechanical components to clog and fail to operate. Periodic cleaning will prevent this problem.

Line cords are seldom damaged because the appliance is usually not moved around much. Always unplug the toaster from the wall outlet before you attempt to remove a stuck slice of bread, and keep in mind that heating elements can be damaged if you use a knife carelessly to remove a crumpled piece of bread.

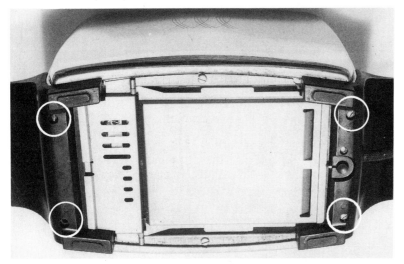

Fig. 39-2. To get into this toaster, remove the four recessed screws in the base.

Fig. 39-3. Next remove the two small screws attaching the crumb tray.

Fig. 39-4. The contacts and connections to the thermostat control are revealed.

Fig. 39-5. For further disassembly, use a small screwdriver to remove the control knob.

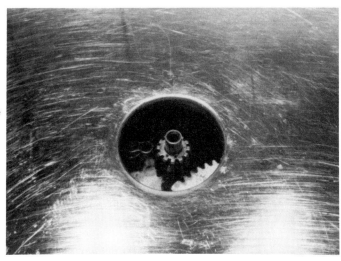

Fig. 39-6. With the knob removed, you can see the main timing gear.

Fig. 39-7. To remove the toaster cover, remove the two retaining screws in the bottom and very carefully lift off the cover.

Fig. 39-8. Once the cover is removed, you can see the line cord connections. The straps going away from the terminals are actually conductors. They carry current and must be insulated from the frame.

Fig. 39-9. On the opposite end of the cord connection is the timing assembly. Often a simple cleaning here will keep the toaster operating for years.

Fig. 39-10. When reassembling the toaster and replacing very small screws, it is sometimes easier to insert the screws in the part and then lower the screws to their holes.

Fig. 39-11. When reattaching the base, notice the slotted holes on the end. They must be aligned with the screws in the base for proper assembly.

VACUUM CLEANER, CANISTER

The constant use of vacuum cleaners and the competitive nature of the manufacturers demand that these appliances be durable and well made. They all operate on the same principle. A line cord, often retractable, is connected through a control switch to a motor. The motor drives a fan, which creates a suction that picks up dirt and debris and forces it into a porous bag. The bag then traps the debris while the air is forced on through and out of the machine.

On this model, the upright portion is actually an attachment. The canister part contains the bag and motor assembly. The control switch is usually reliable, and most problems occur with the line cord or the rewind mechanism. Eventually, the motor brushes could need attention, but by far the most common problem will be a clogged suction hose. First reverse the ends of the hose and turn on the vacuum. If this fails to clear the obstruction, try a broom handle or bend a small hook on a straightened coat hanger to fish it out.

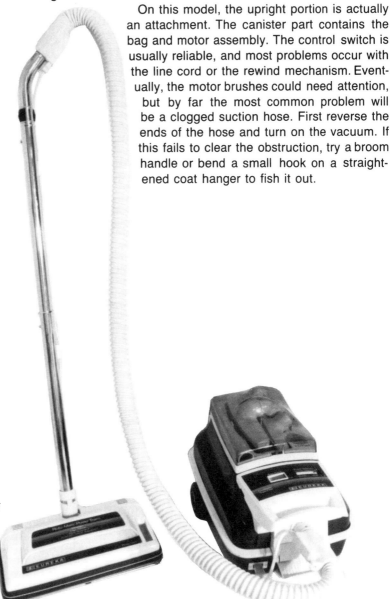

Fig. 40-1. Vacuum cleaner, canister type with upright attachment.

Fig. 40-2. To open up the canister, begin by removing the pin from the hinge of the foot pedal.

Fig. 40-3. Next remove the two screws in the hinge bracket that hold the bag bracket inside the canister. Then carefully lift out the bag and bracket.

Fig. 40-4. Top view showing bag and motor filter. Inspect the filter and the grill over the motor for debris.

Fig. 40-5. To continue disassembling, remove the two screws located on the outside of the canister above the rear wheels. Now lift out the plate holding the motor and cord winder.

Fig. 40-6. Bottom view of the motor and cord winder.

Fig. 40-7. Next remove the four screws holding the brush holder and brushes. Gently pry the wire connectors from the brush holders.

Fig. 40-8. View of the motor showing the brush assemblies removed.

Fig. 40-9. The motor is connected to the plate by four shock-mounted screws.

Fig. 40-10. Remove the three screws on the top side of the plate and lift out the cord winder.

Fig. 40-11. The cord return assembly removed from the plate.

Fig. 40-12. To remove the switch, remove the nut from the outside of the housing, then simply push the switch through.

Fig. 40-13. The switch removed from the housing.

VACUUM CLEANER, UPRIGHT ATTACHMENT

Problems with an upright vacuum are the same as for the canister model, except for troubles associated with the belt and rotary brushes in the vacuum head. The most common problem will be with a jammed brush or a worn belt that slips and fails to turn the brush.

With any vacuum cleaner, there is a temptation to jerk the cord to unplug it from the wall outlet, rather than removing it with the plug. This practice will almost guarantee a faulty line cord.

Fig. 41-1. Vacuum cleaner, upright attachment.

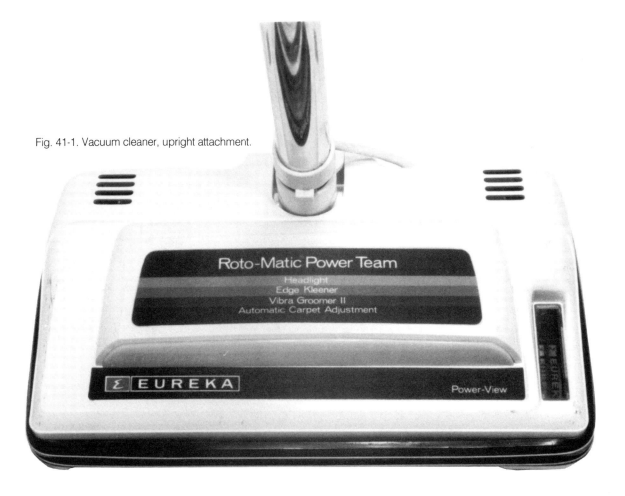

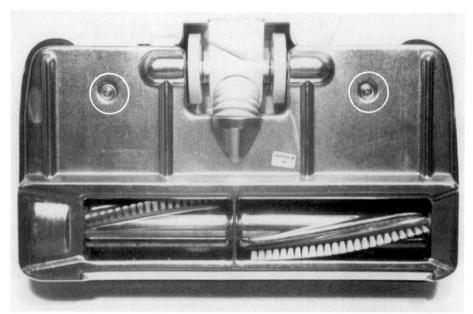

Fig. 41-2. To get inside, remove the two Phillips screws holding on the bottom plate.

Fig. 41-3. With the plate removed, inspect the brushes and belt.

Fig. 41-4. Next remove the two Phillips screws on the bracket holding the motor in place.

Fig. 41-5. Then remove the Phillips screws located on each side of the wheels. They keep the wheels in their compartments.

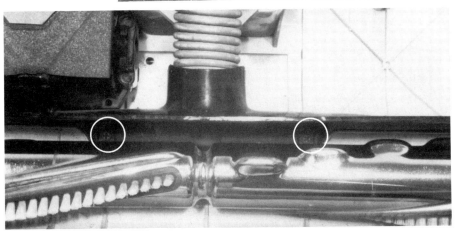

Fig. 41-6. Next remove the two Phillips screws that hold on the back of the brush housing. They also hold on the top cover, which you must remove if the bulb needs to be replaced.

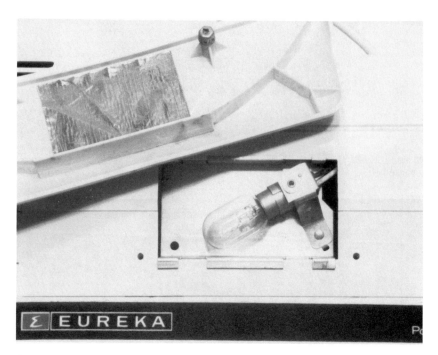

Fig. 41-7. With the cover removed, you have access to the bulb.

Fig. 41-8. At this point, lift out the motor for inspection.

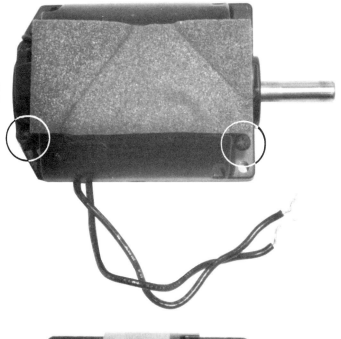

Fig. 41-9. To check out the motor, remove the four Phillips screws and gently separate the two halves.

Fig. 41-10. Now lift out the motor winding and the armature, as well as the bearing and brushes.

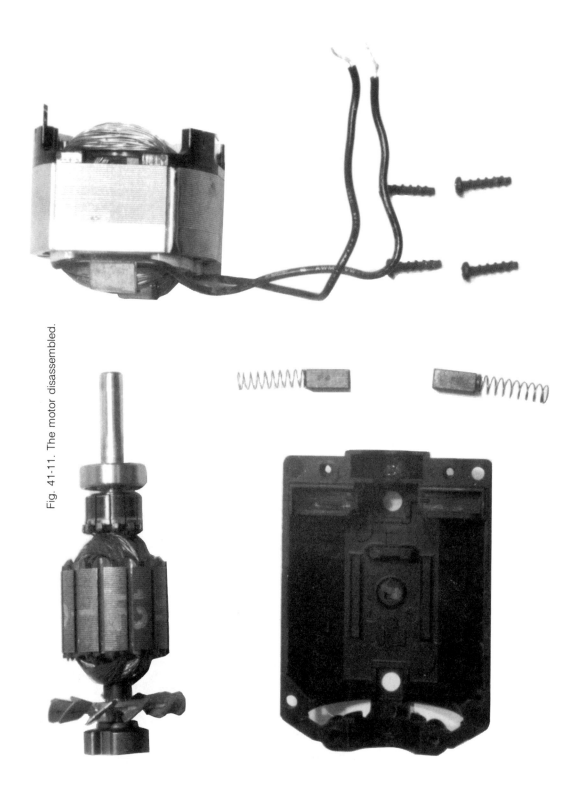

Fig. 41-11. The motor disassembled.

VACUUM, RECHARGEABLE

This small hand vacuum is used mostly for cleaning the carpet in the car; however, it is also very useful for small, quick cleanups around the home. Rechargeable appliances consist of the same components as the ones with the line cord. The difference is that the rechargeable ones are powered by rechargeable batteries.

Rechargeable appliances include a small step-down transformer that plugs into the appliance to keep the batteries recharged. These batteries are not conventional dry cells, which cannot be recharged, but are usually nickel-cadmium batteries, which are rechargeable.

These appliances operate on a lower voltage. They seldom have the problems associated with the arcing and burning of contacts that occur with appliances using a higher voltage.

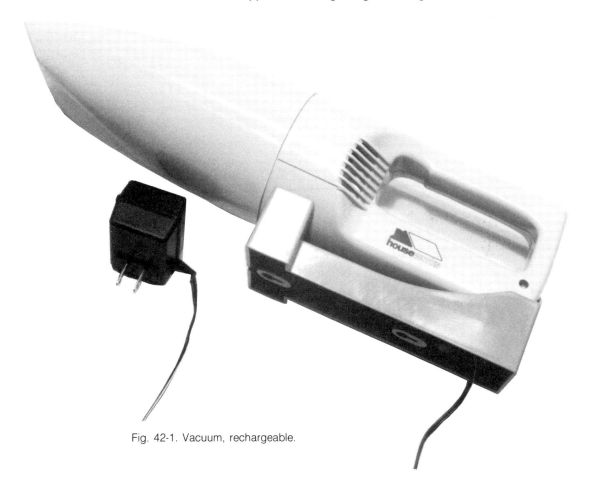

Fig. 42-1. Vacuum, rechargeable.

Fig. 42-2. The front housing is held in place by a twist lock. To begin disassembly, twist the front housing slightly and remove it. This will expose the plate containing the dust filter.

Fig. 42-3. The dust filter is a small bag held in place by an elastic retaining band.

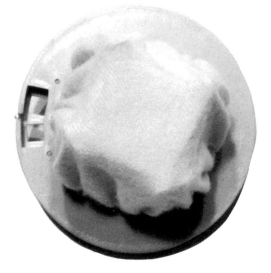

Fig. 42-4. The dust filter and bracket removed from the housing.

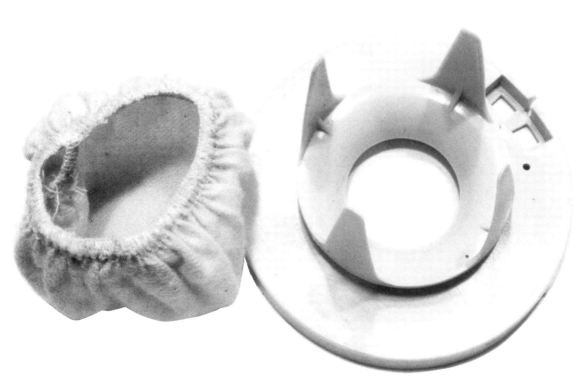

Fig. 42-5. The dust filter removed from the bracket.

Fig. 42-6. Inside the front of the housing is a rubber flapper that allows dirt to be sucked in, but closes when the motor is shut off, preventing the dirt from falling back out.

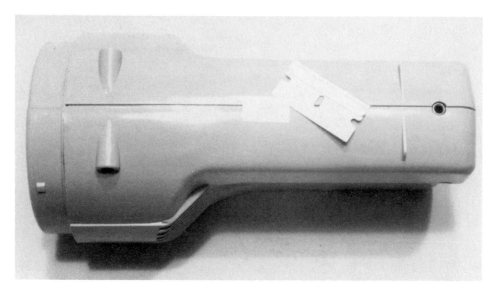

Fig. 42-7. To get inside the main part of the housing, peel off the decal located on the bottom.

Fig. 42-8. Next remove the two Phillips screws located on the side of the appliance. They hold the two halves of the housing together.

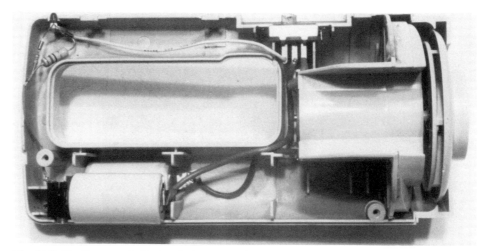

Fig. 42-9. Gently separate the two halves, exposing the battery pack, switch, and indicator lamp. There are no screws holding these components in place. This inside view shows the switch and wiring to the motor and batteries.

Fig. 42-10. The plug connection for the recharging cord.

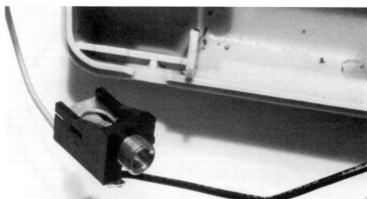

Fig. 42-11. You can remove the battery pack (*shown*), along with the rest of the components individually and inspect them, or you can lift out the entire assembly from its housing. Notice the position of each component, because they will have to go back in the same notches when you reassemble, and there are no screw holes to use as guides.

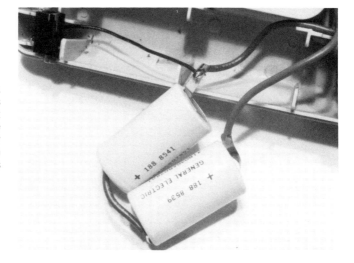

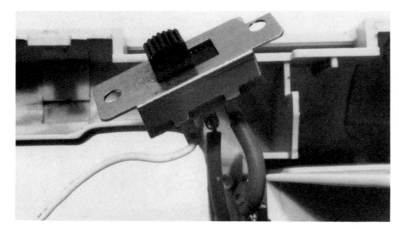

Fig. 42-12. The switch is held in place by the lip on the housing.

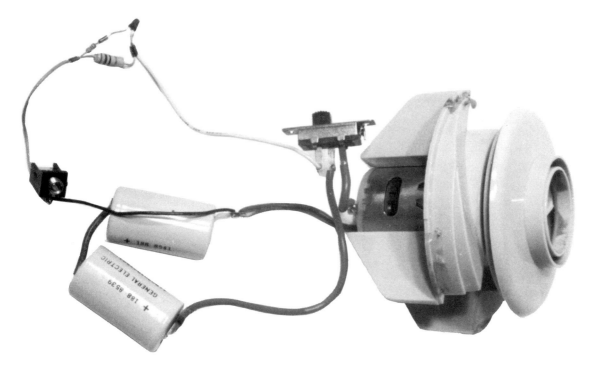

Fig. 42-13. The motor assembly removed from the housing.

WOK

An electric wok normally doesn't receive the day-to-day use associated with other small appliances, so consequently, it offers little troubles. This appliance is basically a heating element with a detachable line cord. It has an adjustable thermostat, which allows the temperature to be regulated. Problems normally associated with this appliance are limited to the thermostat or the heating element itself.

Fig. 43-1. Wok.

Fig. 43-2. Begin by removing the two nuts holding the bottom cover in place.

Fig. 43-3. Next remove the two small nuts inside the plug receptacle holding the plug terminals in place.

Fig. 43-4. With the plate removed, inspect the wiring to the heating element and the control thermostat.

Fig. 43-5. For further disassembly, remove the one nut from the terminal of the heating element. Next, remove the two nuts alongside the thermostat holding the bracket. With the cover removed, lift out the thermostat and the heating element.

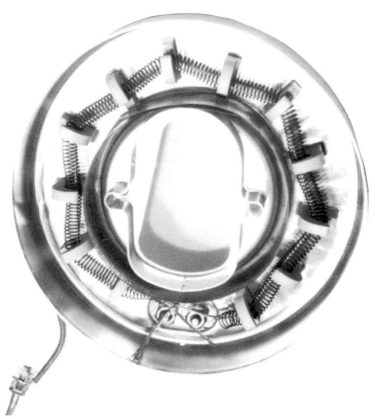

Fig. 43-6. The heating element.

Fig. 43-7. Inspect the thermostat contacts for burning or pitting.

Index